THE MANKIND SERIES OF GREAT ADVENTURES OF HISTORY

The Ancient World

Compiled, edited and with an Introduction
by Raymond Friday Locke

A Mankind Book

MANKIND PUBLISHING COMPANY
LOS ANGELES

THE MANKIND SERIES OF GREAT ADVENTURES OF HISTORY

The Ancient World

"The Age of Solomon," by Marvin Berry, © 1967 by Mankind Publishing Company.

"The Rise of Alcibiades and the Fall of the Athenian Empire," by Rick Kemmer, © 1970 by Mankind Publishing Company.

"The Age of Alexander," by Ronald Leal, © 1969 by Mankind Publishing Company.

"A Legendary View of Alexander," by Ronald Leal, © 1969 by Mankind Publishing Company.

"An Architect for All Ages," by Richard J. Hunter, © 1967 by Mankind Publishing Company.

"Italica: The Romans in Spain," by Sylva E. Mularchyk, © 1970 by Mankind Publishing Company.

"Christianity: From Hunted Sect to State Religion," by Michael Grant, © 1967 by Mankind Publishing Company.

"The Key to the Ancient Mediterranean: Syria, Lebanon and Israel," by Michael Grant, © 1969 by Mankind Publishing Company.

© 1970 by Mankind Publishing Company, 8060 Melrose Avenue, Los Angeles, California. All rights reserved.

Library of Congress Catalog Card Number: 79-135906
SBN: 87687-001-9

Book design by Andrew Furr.

CONTENTS

The Age of Solomon by Marvin Berry	9
The Rise of Alcibiades and the Fall of the Athenian Empire by Rick Kemmer	33
The Age of Alexander by Ronald Leal	57
A Legendary View of Alexander by Ronald Leal	101
The Age of Augustus by Marvin Berry	109
An Architect for All Ages by Richard J. Hunter	155
Pontius Pilate. The Judge Who Changed History by Paul L. Maier	173
The Key to the Ancient Mediterranean: Syria, Lebanon and Israel by Michael Grant	185
Christianity: From Hunted Sect to State Religion by Michael Grant	211
Italica: The Romans in Spain by Sylva E. Mularchyk	231

INTRODUCTION

Having attended schools at which the study of ancient history was not only encouraged but required, I was somewhat amazed to discover recently that in several parts of the United States it is possible for a student to graduate from both high school and college without being exposed to as much as an introductory course in classical history. Not only is it possible for a student of the Space Age to forgo the study of the classics, I am told that a great many of them do. Presumably a knowledge of Homer, of Virgil, of the causes and results of the Peloponnesian War, of Greek law and the beginnings of Christianity are no longer considered pertinent.

Yet the Greeks gave us our law and our concept of democracy, the Latins gave us the root of the major modern languages of the Western World and Christianity has been a prime force in shaping the modern world. Even our present-day concept of history in large part follows the pattern set forth by the classical historians of Greece and Rome. It would seem to me that, even in our highly mechanized society, a knowledge of the very basis, the foundation of our western civilization, with all its fallacies and all its virtues, is most relevant.

The ten pieces contained in this journal were selected with a sense of relevance in mind. Five of them deal directly with events that, or people who became pivotal points in ancient history: King Solomon; Alcibiades and the Peloponnesian War; Alexander's conquest and his spreading Greek culture to Asia; Augustus and the stabilization of the Roman Empire; and Pontius Pilate and the crucifixion of Christ. The other five essays are generally broader in scope but no less pertinent in content. They deal with an architect who lived two thousand years ago and who conceived in his mind and writings much of what is regarded as "new" in contemporary architecture; the legendary lore that came to surround a great soldier and statesman; Christianity and how it progressed from a hunted sect to a state religion; the building and functions of a Roman colonial city; and as timely as today's newspaper, the seeds of conflict that have surfaced periodically throughout the long history of Syria, Lebanon and Israel, a conflict that continues into tomorrow but, to date, has held few surprises for the student of ancient history.

RAYMOND FRIDAY LOCKE
Editor, Mankind Magazine

CONTRIBUTORS

Marvin Berry is associate professor of history and classics at the University of Southern California. A native of South Carolina, he was a Woodrow Wilson Fellow at Princeton and received his Ph.D. from the University of North Carolina.

A former national president of Eta Sigma Phi, National Classics Honorary Fraternity, Rick Kemmer is associate editor of *Insulation* magazine and a graduate of Marquette University.

A young scholar first published by MANKIND magazine, Ronald Leal has since published in scholarly journals in the United States and Latin America. He is a graduate of the University of Mexico.

A former associate professor of architecture at Pennsylvania State University, Richard J. Hunter is now a practicing architect in Los Angeles.

Paul L. Maier is professor of ancient history at Western Michigan University and author of the book *Pontius Pilate*.

Michael Grant is universally acknowledged as one of the most eminent scholars of the classical Roman era and has published twelve books on the ancient world. He is former president and vice-chancellor of the Queen's University, Belfast, Northern Ireland.

Sylva E. Mularchyk is a career civil service employee and freelance writer who lives in Spain.

THE AGE OF SOLOMON

By Marvin Berry

No name in the annals of ancient history is more familiar to modern man than that of Solomon, the King of Israel. His wealth, wisdom, and wives are proverbial. His court evokes in the modern imagination a picture of grandeur unparalleled. While these general thoughts come to mind at the mention of his name, few could tell when Solomon lived, what the circumstances of his reign were, or why he acquired the acclaim that has emblazoned his name on all successive generations.

A proper understanding of Solomon's life and times requires a brief historical orientation. It would be impossible to render judgments on the king's successes and failures without an awareness of his own personal background or of the factors that so greatly influenced the lives and thoughts of the people over whom he ruled. What were the circumstances that had brought the Hebrews forth under Solomon as a mighty people? What were their origins and what had occurred by Solomon's time to make them so significant a nation?

Solomon came to the throne of Israel around 960 B.C. As long ago as this may seem, it was very late in the annals of the achievements of ancient powers. Twenty-two centuries before Solomon, Egypt had risen as a mighty kingdom and was for two thousand years a power unequaled in the ancient Middle East. Fifteen centuries before Solomon, strong rulers had formed empires in Mesopotamia. Six hundred years before Solomon, a robust people, the Hittites, had forged a nation in Asia Minor (modern Turkey), aided in this by their discovery and use of iron. When in the tenth century Solomon brought his people into a position of international eminence he was, in fact, a johnny-come-lately.

The earliest stories involving the Hebrews are concerned with three patriarchs: Abraham, Isaac and Jacob. Abraham had migrated to Palestine from Ur, a large, impressive Mesopotamian metropolis in Chaldea. In Palestine Abraham lived out his life, and there his descendants Isaac and Jacob continued to reside.

Few details have come down to us about Isaac, but Jacob's place in these early traditions is interesting. He deceived his father Isaac in order to receive the important patriarchal blessing and thereby gained ascendancy over his older twin brother Esau. Esau's justified anger at this deceit caused Jacob to flee from Palestine to northern Mesopotamia. Living there for about twenty years he prospered; he became wealthy and produced a large family of his own. When he finally returned to his original home in Palestine his name was changed to Israel, making him the eponymous ancestor of the Hebrews. His twelve sons became the eponymous ancestors of the twelve particular tribes, although Joseph's two sons, Ephraim and Manasseh, supplanted to names of Joseph and the priestly clan of Levi.

The familiar story of the sale of Joseph into Egypt is concerned with the last major patriarchal tradition. Ten of Joseph's brothers were so inflamed by Jacob's preference for Joseph and Joseph's brother Benjamin that they contemplated murdering Joseph. However, upon meeting merchants en route to Egypt, they decided to rid themselves of Joseph by selling him.

This malicious sale was to prove to be a blessing. Joseph prospered in Egypt; he won the favor of the Pharaoh and was made *grand vizier*, or Prime Minister, of Egypt. In this position he was overseer of the food supply, an important role in times of food crises or shortages. As often happened in ancient Palestine, a famine struck. Jacob realized that the bounty of Egypt could sustain him and his family at the time of this emergency. Therefore, he sent his ten oldest sons to Egypt to procure grain.

Unaware that Joseph, their brother, was in a powerful position, the brothers went to purchase grain. Joseph recognized them but did not reveal his identity. Testing them to see how they felt now toward his own brother Benjamin, Joseph ascertained that the former feelings of hatred were gone. Only then did he reveal his identity and a joyful reunion occurred. Joseph secured the permission of the Pharaoh to bring his entire family to reside in Egypt. Jacob and his whole clan came and were given the most prized agricultural region, the Delta, in which to reside.

This warm reception in Egypt is interesting and puzzling. It is known that the Egyptians loathed the dirty Bedouin shepherds from the desert regions. How did it happen that the government not only welcomed the Bedouin clan of Jacob but gave to those immigrants the most fertile area of Egypt as their home?

THE AGE OF SOLOMON

Around 1785 B.C. the native Egyptian dynasty was overthrown by an invasion of shepherds from the eastern desert areas. For two centuries these despised invaders, known as the "Shepherd Kings," ruled Egypt from the stranglehold over the land brought about by their firm control of the fertile Delta of the Nile Valley. It is generally believed that Jacob and his family could have migrated to Egypt during the period of these shepherd kings. This easily explains why Joseph and Jacob could have been so heartily welcomed.

About two hundred years later in 1580 B.C. the shepherd kings were overthrown. The new native rulers, fearing the alien residents and the trouble they might create, immediately enslaved them and put them to work as laborers in enormous building programs. Until a dynamic leader, Moses, came forth and effected his people's escape, the Hebrew slaves toiled for the Pharaoh. Biblical authorities date this deliverance, or Exodus, from Egypt around 1290 to 1220 B.C.

The story of the Exodus became one of the most significant traditions in the early history of the Hebrews. No nation in antiquity, save this one, looked upon itself as one arising originally from abject bondage. So unusual did it seem that an escape from the mightiest empire in ancient times was possible, one can easily understand how the traditions concerning the release grew and abounded in awesome details: the opening of the seas, the guiding cloud of fire, the providential gifts of manna, quail, and water. But the slaves did escape and hurriedly marched eastward out of reach of Egyptian forces.

As soon as a safe spot around Mt. Sinai was reached, the fugitives rested and reflected on the incomprehensible events which they had just experienced. No explanation for this turn of fortune seemed to them possible unless it was that some divine Agent had helped them. It seemed that He was bringing them forth to make them His own people. At Mt. Sinai the escaped slaves determined that this was the case and, in a solemn covenant, they dedicated themselves to this divine Power, the God who they believed had saved them, and the One whom, they thought, their forebears had worshipped. As an indication of how closely they felt their God had been acting on their behalf, they gave to Him a personal name, Yahweh, which is translated into English as Jehovah or Lord.

Filled with a sense of dedication and meaning, the slaves were transformed into a people with a purpose. They had a Deity with whom they had covenanted to worship. They had their leader Moses, who acted as a spokesman for their God. Most significantly they had the feeling that each of them, regardless of his rank or position, was equal before this Deity whom they had accepted as their own. He was their King and they were all equal subjects before Him. They had, in fact, established for themselves a theocratic government, a government where their God was their King. From Mt. Sinai the people began to march toward Palestine, the land where their ancestors had once lived.

Palestine, or Canaan, as it is called in the Biblical text, was an area situated at the southwestern end of the cradle of many ancient civilizations. From Neolithic times the Palestinian-Phoenician-Syrian area had been the center of cultures rivaling, only on a smaller scale, the progress made in Egypt and Mesopotamia. It was a critical, pivotal area because it was and would be for centuries to come the land link between Egypt and Mesopotamia.

So eager were all ancient empires to possess this "bridge" that Palestine was the scene of constant, innumerable military contests: Egypt continually sought possession of it as a shield for herself from any invader; other kingdoms viewed it as the springboard for an invasion of the fertile, wealthy Nile Valley. Only once in

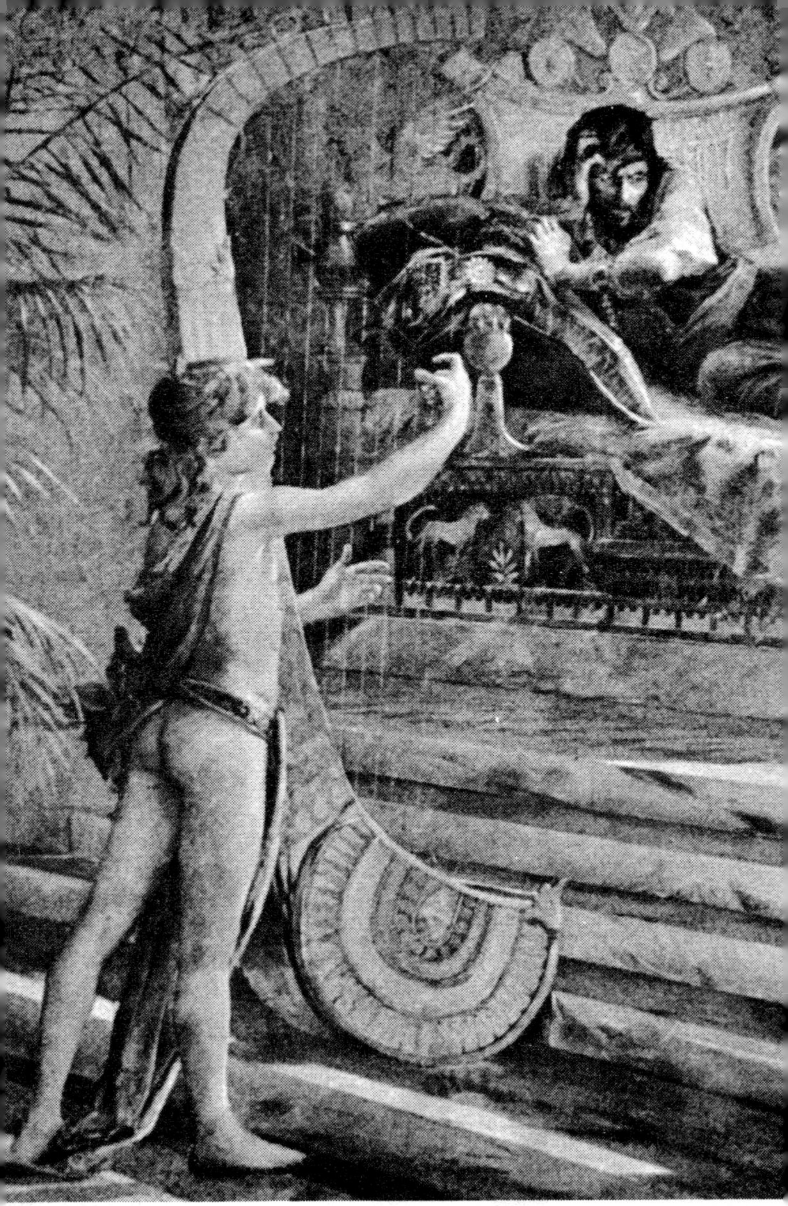

David calming the wrath of Saul

antiquity was Palestine to be relatively secure from foreign threats and international intrigues. This was during the reign of Solomon.

Wandering through the barren wastelands of the Sinai peninsula was a trying period for the Hebrews after they had escaped the bondage of the Pharaoh. Two factors, however, sustained them: the conviction that Yahweh was with them and the gradual increase in their ranks as friendly, related desert tribes joined them on the march. When they had come to the Jordan Valley and were ready to march into Palestine, Moses died. A new, energetic leader, Joshua, took Moses' place and tradition ascribes to his leadership the initial invasion of Canaan.

The wandering clans found that their destination, the "land of milk and honey," would be a most difficult region to conquer. Strong, seemingly impregnable cities had been built by the native inhabitants and surrounded every desirable site. The natives did not intend to surrender to the invaders from the eastern desert.

The difficulties in taking Palestine led to the scattering of the invading tribes; they could not maintain themselves as a unit but were forced to live wherever they could dislodge any of the entrenched natives. Gradually the invaders began to infiltrate the mountainous backbone that ran the length of the country. After two hundred years of such scattered guerrilla activity the original tribes had little in common. Only two factors held these Hebrews together: a vague sense of unity under the Deity whom they and their forebears had worshipped and the constant threat from coalitions of native chiefs who attempted to repossess the area taken by them.

Around the eleventh century another factor entered the picture. A militant, capable "people from the sea" invaded the southwestern coast of Palestine. These invaders quickly consolidated their hold along the coast and began to move inland. They came quickly into contact with the Hebrews who were, at the same time, attempting to move out of the mountains into the coastal plains. The ensuing conflict is one of the most familiar to us: the confrontation between the Hebrews and the Philistines.

This was a crisis that became a turning point in Hebrew history. Faced with annihilation from this common threat, the tribes turned to the famous Samuel, who managed for the moment to stop the Philistine invasion of the mountain strongholds. As Samuel grew older, though, the threat was still ominous. Realizing this, the tribes demanded a strong leader to succeed Samuel. They asked him to give them a king. Samuel, aghast, reminded them that in such a request they were breaking the covenant made at Sinai. He told them that a king would impose a severe hand upon them. A king might tax, conscript, and in other ways curb their individual rights. They persisted in their demand. Reluctantly Samuel chose the handsome, regal Saul to become the first King of the Hebrews.

And an unfortunate choice it was. Saul was mentally deranged. He suffered continually from extreme melancholy, a condition which precluded his success in the two areas where, at this time, it was imperative for the leader to succeed. Because of this affliction he was not able to unite the people and, therefore, could only contain, not obliterate, the Philistine threat.

To confound his tenuous position the king alienated Samuel and the groups who maintained a longing for the return to a theocratic government when he attempted to assert his own authority. He began to disobey Samuel's injunctions. Samuel then denounced him, declaring that the kingdom would be taken from him. For a man already walking a mental tightrope this estrangement with the revered Samuel made it impossible for the king to proceed with a consistent policy or with the loyalty of his people.

While the relationship between Saul and Samuel was deteriorating, troubles were developing in the royal household over the friendship between the Crown Prince Jonathan and a shepherd boy, David, who had been brought into the king's house to soothe the troubled mind of Saul with music. The king, in a state of extreme melancholia, felt that David was attempting to secure for himself the royal power and thus subvert the dynasty which Saul hoped to establish. When Jonathan made a chance remark that David would make a capable king, and when the crowds sang more loudly David's praises than they sang Saul's, the enraged king attempted to murder David.

David was forced to flee into the Judaean wilderness, taking with him a band of loyal followers. Saul pursued, his mental anguish increasing. Throughout the time of this ordeal David manifested continuing loyalty to the mad king, even forbidding his men to harm the king in any way. At the same time, David's following increased. Moved by his plight; many of the common people aided David by hiding him, by giving provisions to him and his men, and by joining his band.

Saul persisted in the internecine struggle, debilitating the strength of the people with this wasteful expenditure of energy. The Philistines noted this and began to take advantage of the disunity among the Hebrews. Upon hearing that the enemy had massed around the mountains to the north, Saul rushed to meet the threat. Amidst the mountains of Gilboa Saul's army met a disastrous defeat. The king was slain along with Jonathan and two other sons.

Immediately the southern part of the country, that area from which David had come and in which he was so familiar, declared David king. The northern tribes acknowledged a young son of Saul, Ishbosheth, as their new ruler. This division, ominously similar to what would happen after Solomon's death, again jeopardized the position of the tribes before the Philistine threat.

Over the next few years, however, David's position grew steadily stronger. The loyalty of the northern tribes turned more and more toward him as Ishbosheth's influence waned. Finally, Saul's son was murdered by two of his own commanders who hoped to ingratiate themselves before David. David immediately executed the assassins and showed magnanimity to the surviving members of Saul's house. The door was now opened for unity. The northern tribes pledged fealty to David and acknowledged him as their king.

Within Israel itself David began to organize his kingdom. With his strong army he was able to maintain peace within his borders as well as without. He gathered around him a bureaucracy, small at first but destined to grow larger, to enable him to govern efficiently. Even so there were violent dissensions within his own family. His son Absolom attempted to overthrow him. Several discontented northerners raised the cry of rebellion. They were, however, more hostile to the growing entrenchment of power in Jerusalem, David's capital, than they were hostile to David. Because of his sincere personality and because of his ability to remember that he once was a "commoner," the king was successful in maintaining a generally peaceful realm.

David had set about at once to meet the threat of hostile neighbors. As so often happens, it is difficult to stop the march once one enters upon the road of conquest. David was to spend most of his reign subduing every bordering nation. He placed the Philistines under his firm control; he conquered Moab, Edom, Ammon and Assyria. His borders extended finally from the Mediterranean Sea into the Arabian Desert and from the area of the Philistine cities in the south to the Euphrates River in the north.

The quick expansion of the Hebrews over such a

THE AGE OF SOLOMON

large area seems at first glance unusual. One fact, however, explains it: No people in the Middle East at this time was powerful enough to interfere. Egypt, only a century before David, had lapsed into a period of weakness from which she would never in ancient times recover. To the north of Palestine the future empire of Assyria was engaged in overcoming the vestiges of Hittite power and had no interest in matters to her south. In Mesopotamia chaos had reigned since the fall of Hammurabi's dynasty in the eighteenth century B.C. No challenging power would rise there until Nebuchadnezzar came forth at the end of the seventh century B.C.

This, then, was the background of the Hebrew people over whom Solomon would rule: a people only recently united and made secure by David's genius; a people free for the first time from any external threat; a people devoted to their own national deity; a people who wished to enjoy the blessings of a peace they had so recently won. How unfortunate it was for the Hebrews to have a new king who would not live up to their expectations.

Solomon succeeded to the throne under revealing and significant circumstances. David lay dying. The court realized this, and intrigues between various factions in David's family developed. David's oldest son, Adonijah, hastily proclaimed himself the new ruler, aided in this by the commander of David's armies, Joab, and by one of David's priestly advisors, Abiathar. Another court faction, composed of Solomon's mother, Bathsheba, and one of David's close religious "advisors," Nathan, hurriedly went to David's bedside and secured his support for Solomon. In his undoubted senility, unaware of the full implications of what he was doing, David ordered that his son Solomon be proclaimed king.

Aware of widespread opposition and aware that

King Solomon

THE AGE OF SOLOMON

Adonijah had, as David's oldest son, a reasonable claim to the throne, Solomon acted quickly to secure his position. Before his enemies could consolidate their forces Solomon lashed forth. He had Adonijah and Joab murdered, he exiled the religious leaders who had sided with Adonijah, and he restricted the movements of any whom he feared might incite trouble. He allowed no questioning of his power and he resorted to any means to maintain his control. This initial expression of a personal, selfish desire for power was to permeate Solomon's entire reign.

Solomon began to consolidate his power by means of a rigid reorganization of the kingdom. Twelve districts were established to be supervised by royal officials, two of whom were Solomon's sons-in-law. These districts were designated to supply monthly the prerequisites of the royal court in monies, food, material, and labor battalions. The king showed an astuteness in this endeavor, if one may call "astute" those actions designed to weaken any opposition. The newly created districts cut across the traditional tribal borders and loyalties. This was obviously done to render ineffectual all tribal hostility to the growing bureaucracy in Jerusalem.

To the undoubted consternation of the kingdom, the king exempted the district of Judah from the severe demands imposed on the rest of the nation. In this way the king strengthened the loyalty of the region from which his father and he had come. This exemption of the area in which the king and his government resided kept Solomon disastrously unaware of the conditions existing throughout the rest of his realm. He received nothing but praise from a fawning, privileged court which was living off the sweat and toil of their brothers; he heard nothing of the growing resentment and animosity toward him and the centralized government. The rest of the kingdom viewed with alarm the encroachmen of royal authority, an encroachment that unabashedly violated the spirit of equality of all before Yahweh that had been inherent in the covenant made at Sinai.

To strengthen his royal authority abroad the king entered into alliances with neighboring princes and kings. Daughters of rulers from Moab, Egypt, Edom, and the Hittites soon were in Jerusalem. The Biblical text states that in the end Solomon had seven hundred wives and three hundred concubines, a likely exaggeration but a revealing one: One thousand was to the ancients a perfect number. Solomon, as a "perfect" man, had to prove his perfection with this large harem. Regardless of the exact number there were many foreign wives who demanded, and received, their respective palaces and places for worshipping their traditional dieties. The religious scruples of the time did not preclude Solomon's joining his wives in their worship. It was obligatory that he participate; he could not offend the countries from which his wives had come. Soon the shocked Hebrews saw their king participating in rites forbidden in the worship of Yahweh.

To accommodate the influx of aliens and to make the capital city of Jerusalem the most luxurious one possible, Solomon undertook a building program of gigantic proportions. It was partly concerned with the residences of his wives, but was primarily involved with his own quarters. For thirteen years laborers worked on his personal palace and the citadel connected with it. Other sites in his kingdom were beautified and strengthened: the important pass at Megiddo, the strategic site at Hazor, and the important port of Gezer on the Red Sea.

One building, Solomon's temple, requires a special note. The Biblical text devotes a disproportionate amount of information to describing it. A careful scrutiny, however, can put the temple in a more just light. It was a minor project compared to others. It required only seven years to build, roughly half the time needed for Solomon's palace, and it seems to have been a mere appendage to the palace. It was sumptuously decorated, to be sure, but it would hardly have been more magnificent than the scores of other buildings constructed around Jerusalem. The minute details of description seem to indicate that the devotees of Yahweh took heart that it was built at all, in view of the many other buildings and in view of Solomon's growing laxity in maintaining the worship of Yahweh as the state religion.

In constructing the temple complex Solomon obtained the assistance of Hiram, the Phoenician king of Tyre. From Hiram came artisans and materials, especially the famous cedars of Lebanon. For a heavy price Solomon received these services, and the resulting temple most certainly was a disappointment to many. One could not have distinguished it from many other Phoenician-Canaanite buildings and temples, and the expense added greatly to the exorbitant costs of the luxurious court.

The king's harem, military fortresses, palaces, and court required an enormous income, even by modern standards. The small kingdom, in times of extreme prosperity, would have found the expense of the royal government a difficult yoke to bear. The heavy taxation imposed on the land, however, met only a part of the necessary expenses. To obtain additional revenues, the king assumed a royal monopoly over the caravan routes throughout his borders. This provided an important source of revenue since all caravans going north or south had to journey through Palestine.

A third source of wealth was also tapped. The king began to exploit the copper resources around the Red Sea. Again, Hiram sent aid; he furnished Solomon with ships and seamen to enable Solomon to build up a large merchant marine corps. So successful was this enterprise that Solomon could rightly be called the first "Copper Baron" of antiquity.

It is probably due to this commercial activity along the Red Sea that the Queen of Sheba came on a state visit to Jerusalem. The Biblical narrator cannot say enough about the significance of this visit. In the eyes of the writer Solomon's name was known and praised by all who were familiar with his court. In the narrative, though, one can detect that Solomon was not particularly expert in this one diplomatic endeavor; the queen obtained all that she desired from the King of Israel!

It is feasible to suspect that the king could not afford troubles in that southern area of his sphere of influence; he was facing rebellion by several captive states around him. Both Damascus and Edom threw off the yoke of Solomon, thereby endangering the king's revenue from caravans.

Finally, the king realized that he could not maintain his court in the accustomed fashion and at the same time pay his creditors their due. Hiram, for one, was becoming anxious concerning the debts owed him. Solomon, to Hiram's displeasure, ceded the area of Galilee to him. The Phoenician would have preferred payment in gold or silver.

As the king entered the last days of his reign he could look about and see the chaos he had produced. He had bled his people in taxes and he had caused dissension within and rebellion without. He had alienated the majority of his subjects because of the insensitive despotism of the court. Born to the purple and accustomed to privileges, the king was in no position to view closely the attitudes and feelings of his people. The greater tragedy is that, in his personal arrogance and desire for absolute power, he made no attempt to know his people. Solomon had lost completely the touch with the masses that had made David's reign significant and,

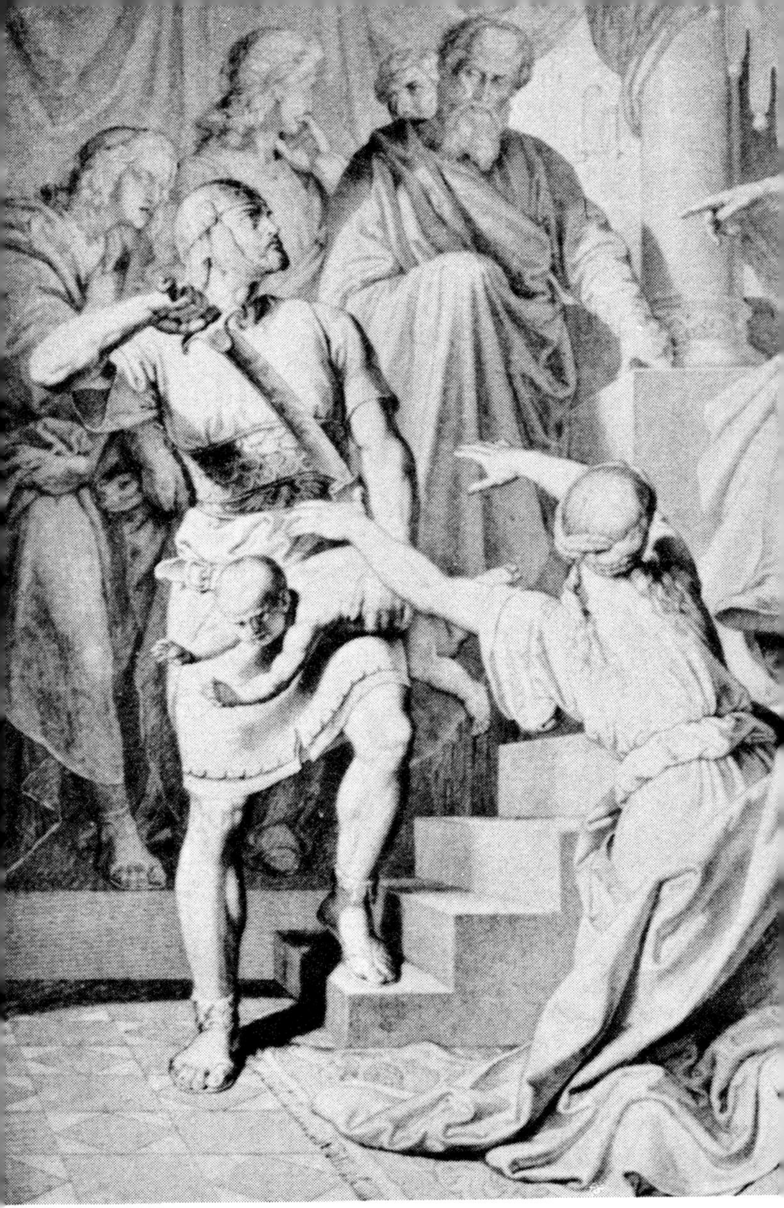

The judgment of Solomon

indeed, possible.

The king had also precluded a lasting, peaceful union of tribes by resorting to his measures of outright force with an utter lack of understanding of the temperament of the northern area. His ruthless tax program, his corvee system employed for the ambitious public works, his sumptuous court—all of these contrasted with the simplicity and poverty of the northern farmers and made the north rebel at the first opportunity. A leader, Jeroboam, led an abortive attempt; he escaped Solomon's wrath by fleeing to Egypt. Later, under Solomon's son Rehoboam, he was to be more successful and was to become Jeroboam I, the first important king of the northern kingdom.

In the midst of internal and external problems Solomon died. His son Rehoboam had no sooner assumed the crown than he was confronted with an embassy from the northern tribes. Its mission was a simple one: to ask the new king to listen to their grievances and to change the abusive policies of his father. If he would do this, they said, they would gladly continue to serve him. Rehoboam dismissed the petitioners, telling them to return later for his answer.

The young king sought the opinion of his advisors. His older counselors, aware of the destructive nature of Solomon's policies, urged the king to heed the northern tribesmen's requests. The younger advisors, as spoiled and insensitive as Solomon had been and as Rehoboam would prove to be, urged the king to assert himself. Unhappily Rehoboam accepted this latter advice. He warned the petitioners that he would add to their yoke and that his force and might would be much heavier for them than his father's had been. This incident presents the best picture possible of Solomon's failure as both a king and a father.

When external forces are most pressing the inner man's true self often appears. It did on this occasion.

THE AGE OF SOLOMON

The Hebrews, under Solomonic oppression, had not forgotten the basic tenet of the equality of them all before Yahweh. It was the bureaucratic court that had forgotten.

At this reply from Rehoboam a shout of defiant rebellion was heard throughout the kingdom, the same shout that David and Solomon had both heard. Rehoboam attempted to put down the rebellion by force. He sent the hated slave battalion leaders into the seceding areas. They were stoned to death by the enraged tribesmen who chose the fugitive Jeroboam as their leader and king. Most of the kingdom turned to him and retained the name of the Kingdom of Israel. Only Judah, the privileged center of the Solomonic era, remained loyal to Rehoboam.

In truth Solomon had led his people to the pinnacle of position and power. But in so doing he had created the forces that later were to rise up and pull into ruins the entire political fabric. The division of the kingdom can be attributed directly to Solomon's policies. This division ultimately so weakened the Hebrews that they were in no position to withstand the future onslaught of imperialistic powers. While it would be improper to speculate about what might have happened had the nation maintained its unity, it is a historical fact that two small, independent, and often antagonistic kingdoms in this critical geographical location were no match for the powers of Assyria, Babylon, and Persia.

In spite of the overwhelming evidence that Solomon's vanity and love of luxury had ruined his people one seldom, if ever, hears anythings but praise for this selfish king. Again there is an explanation, and it is a simple one.

During the four centuries that followed Solomon's reign the Hebrews were subjected to the attacks of each of the successive imperial powers in the Middle East. The militaristic power of Assyria obliterated the northern kingdom of Israel two centuries after it had been established. Assyria attempted, unsuccessfully, to overcome the mountain strongholds of Judah. The Neo-Babylonian empire under Nebuchadnezzar defeated the Assyrians at the end of the seventh century and succeeded in conquering Judah. The population of the small kingdom was deported to Babylon to prevent any opposition from arising and remained there until the Persians defeated Babylon and freed the Judeans.

During these many years of national calamity and destruction the Judeans had little hope. They constantly had to struggle to maintain their identity, often with small success, amidst the foreign powers with whom they were coming into contact. They began to attach more and more significance to the temple edifice built by Solomon, which became for them a symbol both of their national Deity and of their glorious past. Even when it had been destroyed their hopes could not be extricated from the fervent desire that the temple be rebuilt. The temple, and the God of that temple, were for them the distinguishing marks in the periods of upheaval.

As these dejected Judeans reflected on their present loss of national dignity it was natural that they looked longingly back to that time when they were the strongest power in their world. This had occurred during the reign of their king Solomon, under whom they had been the privileged province. Soon a mystic aura surrounded the life and accomplishments of Solomon. He had made them a political power and he had built the temple for their Deity. Nothing, therefore, but good could be associated with his age.

No better evidence for this can be found than that of the many pieces of literature associated with Solomon's name. The wisdom attributed to Solomon knew no limits. It did not occur to later generations that true wisdom comes from experience, not from selfish, luxurious

THE AGE OF SOLOMON

indulgence.

Solomon's single inadvertent success, then, was only that one of providing his people of a later age with a symbol of hope and meaning. Long after Solomon's oppressive tax measures, his slave labor battalions, and his sumptuous court were forgotten the Hebrews could look back and feel that his age was their one inimitable period of achievement. So still does modern man erroneously view the age of Solomon.

Death of Saul

Alcibiades

THE RISE OF ALCIBIADES AND THE FALL OF THE ATHENIAN EMPIRE

By Rick Kemmer

*T*wentieth century America has ascended to world power only to find herself embroiled in endless war. If, under this constant pressure she splits into unreconcilable factions as over Vietnam, if her course seems to veer perilously from right to left, hawk to dove, she is only exhibiting a common phenomenon of democracy the historian Thucydides recorded 2400 years ago in his *History of the Peloponnesian War*. Unfortunately, we can take little solace from the example of Thucydides' Athens—her conduct was in many ways similar to our own, and it led her to total ruin.

Like our own country, Athens was a volatile democracy. In the years after the Persian war she flowered into Hellas' most beautiful city, her Acropolis crowned by the Parthenon and the Temple of Athene Nike whose reconstructed ruins still enchant travelers with their grace and restraint. Her genius statesman, Pericles, fortified Athens and built long connecting walls to Piraeus, giving her constant access to the sea. An invincible naval power, she became the chief city and protectress of the famous Delian League, which eventually became a far-flung Athenian empire of over one thousand cities including almost all the islands of the Aegean and the cities of Ionia. The wealth and power of the Athenian empire increased daily until it rose to challenge the traditional dominance of Sparta and the Peloponnesian League.

In 431 B.C., rivalry between Sparta and Athens erupted into the Archidamian War, the first stage of what Thucydides called the "Great Peloponnesian War." The war ended in a draw ten years later with a fifty-year alliance engineered by an Athenian aristocrat named Nicias. At that time Athens had consolidated her power. She was equal to Sparta and still striving to be greater.

The "cold war" period that followed saw a young soldier named Alcibiades rise to prominence in the war party at Athens. If ever there was a basis for President John F. Kennedy's observation that "Things do not just happen. They are made to happen. . . ." it was Alcibiades.

As his career unfolded, he renewed the Peloponnesian War. He commanded the Athenian fleet on the grandest expedition ever launched by a Greek city and, defecting to the enemy, turned that expedition into the most costly fiasco of the war. Later he returned to lead the Athenian fleet in a string of victories that nearly swept the Spartans from the seas. He was almost crowned a king in a democracy he at one time helped overthrow and later fought to restore. Historians have branded him amoral, immoral, traitor, dissolute, and countless other epithets, but Alcibiades was in fact the

THE RISE OF ALCIBIADES

very spirit of Athens. He and Athens reached their zenith together after a stormy courtship—and together they tumbled to disaster.

The Athenian public never ceased to wonder at Alcibiades, to argue about him, to criticize and to praise him. And he gave them much to talk about.

He loved to promenade like a woman in flowing purple gowns that dragged on the street as he walked, and he was given to elaborate feasts and continuous revelry. He was the only Athenian ever so extravagant as to enter seven chariots in the Olympic Games. He once punched a leading citizen in the face for no reason other than to win a bet; but such was the magnitude of his personality that he later became the man's close friend and married his daughter. When the girl later sought to divorce him, Alcibiades stormed into the public hearing, flung her over his shoulder like a sack of potatoes, and carried her home. Later Alcibiades fathered an illegitimate child. Against the prevailing custom of his time, he publicly recognized the child as his own and supported him.

In 415 B.C., Alcibiades triggered his fate and the fate of his country by selling Athens on a war to conquer Sicily. It was simple self-interest, he argued. Sicily was ripe for the picking and would serve as a stepping stone to conquest of the whole western Mediterranean. With the west under her control, Sparta would be encircled and could be destroyed.

Alcibiades talked down the opposition of Nicias who contended that Sparta was still the major enemy and that a reverse abroad would enable the Lacedaemonians to attack Athens with her power badly divided. "Even if we do conquer the Sicilians," Nicias warned, "we have nothing to gain. They are too numerous and too far away to be governed."

But with the younger members of the assembly looking for an empire, a cause, and a leader, Alcibiades won the argument. He and Athens catapulted into the maelstrom of a war that lasted twelve years. The Sicilian campaign turned out to be only the first phase, but it constitutes one of the most incredible chapters of democratic bungling, betrayal, and luckless fate in military history.

To achieve a political consensus for attacking Sicily, the Assembly chose Nicias to co-command an armada with Alcibiades and Lamachos, who was an outstanding soldier but whose poverty incurred the disrespect of his men. Although Nicias, still adamantly against the scheme, kept trying to discourage his countrymen by dwelling on the extravagant preparations they needed, he only whetted their enthusiasm. Cavalry, archers, and infantry assembled from all over the empire and the flower of Athenian manhood outfitted itself for the expedition. The fleet was by far the most costly and splendid Hellenic force that had ever been sent out by a single city at one time. Captains and crews vied for honor in adorning their ships with expensive figureheads. Personal fortunes were invested in the trappings.

Even while these preparations were under way, the free-swinging politics of Athenian democracy combined with Alcibiades' controversial personality to undermine ultimate success. One night the *Hermae*, phallic statues that guarded the doors of private homes and temples in the city, were senselessly mutilated. His political opponents, well aware of Alcibiades' penchant for merriment, contrived to blame him for the outrage saying it resulted from one of his drinking parties. Incensed at these unjust accusations, Alcibiades offered to stand trial on the spot and a large portion of his fleet flatly refused to sail to Sicily without him.

Rather than abandon the expedition (after all, it was Alcibiades' war) his enemies temporarily put aside their charges and Alcibiades sailed with the fleet. With the mutilation of the *Hermae* auguring ominously, 134 la-

Praxitele's figure of Hermes playing with the child Dionysus

vishly fitted triremes put to sea carrying 4,000 heavily armed footsoldiers with a multitude of archers and slingers.

Reaching Sicily, they established camp at Catana, a short distance north of Syracuse. Only a few days after they settled, however, the state galley, *Salaminia,* arrived to return Alcibiades to stand trial for his alleged affront to the gods. Graciously the young general consented to follow the *Salaminia* in his own ship, but already making plans for the future, he betrayed the pro-Athenian party in Messana to Syracusan sympathizers and prevented the city from coming over to Athens. When he landed at Thurii in Southern Italy, he disappeared and made his way to Sparta.

Alcibiades' opponents had recalled him to a prejudged execution and he knew it. During his short interval in Sicily, a throng of disreputable never-do-wells were paid to testify that he had profaned the religious mysteries for the entertainment of his friends. Many of his companions were arrested on trumped-up charges and bribed to vilify him or forfeit their lives. How little truth most of the testimony carried was demonstrated by the story of one accuser who claimed he actually saw the faces of the vandals in the moonlight while they went from house to house attacking the statues. This was an unspeakable lie; the sacrilege occurred on the night of the new moon!

Without Alcibiades to prod him, Nicias dallied away the summer without engaging in a conclusive battle. He was quartering at Catana that winter when envoys from Syracuse reached Sparta and found Alcibiades sitting with the council. At first the conservative Spartans refused them aid because they still felt bound by the *Peace of Nicias.* Then Alcibiades asked leave to explain the real purpose of the Athenian presence in Sicily. He told the Spartans:

"We Athenians sailed to Sicily with the design of

subduing first the Greek cities there, and next those of Italy. Then we intended to make an attempt on the dominions of Carthage itself. If all these projects succeeded . . . we intended to increase our fleet with the inexhaustible supplies of ship timber which Italy affords, to put in requisition the whole military force of the conquered Greek states, and to hire large armies of the barbarians, of the Iberians, and others in those regions, who are allowed to make the best possible soldiers. *Then,* when we had done all this, we intended to assail Peloponnesus with our collected force. Our fleets would blockade you by sea and desolate your coasts. Our armies would be landed at different points and assail your cities. Some of these we meant to storm and others we meant to take by surrounding them with fortified lines. We thought that it would thus be an easy matter to thoroughly wear you down; and then we should become the masters of the whole Greek race."

For the first time the shocked Lacedaemonians understood the unbridled designs of Athenian imperialism. Alcibiades went on to suggest countermeasures. It was most urgent, he told them, to send Syracuse a Spartan general as the Sicilian city had no chance to last another summer without someone to direct its army. Sparta responded by sending one of her best generals, Gylippus, to command in Sicily.

In an ironic twist of fate, Alcibiades had been forced to sabotage his own dreams of a western empire. A man of action, he still made things happen. But he seemed to be swimming on a tide of fate that turned his actions to conclusions he never intended. During the next two years no man worked harder to punish the Athenians than he.

As soon as warm weather returned, the Athenian fleet swept ashore in the bay of Thapsus.

The accepted tactic for conquering a town in those days was to encircle it with a double wall so supplies couldn't enter from the outside. With your wall completed, you simply waited until either famine or treachery betrayed the city into your hands. Treachery almost always won the battle for you, for in every city there were democratic and oligarchical factions, one of which was willing to deliver the city for the right price.

Thus, Nicias, who was now ironically first in command, began building a wall from Thapsus on the north, across Epipolae, a high area overlooking the city, to the Great Harbor of Syracuse on the south. At first the Athenians swept all before them, crushing one Syracusan attempt after another to intercept the wall of circumvallation with a cross wall. The Athenians appeared unstoppable. Their army was swelling daily with new allies hoping to share the inevitable spoils. The Athenian wall was almost done and the desperate Syracusans were considering surrender when Gylippus arrived with two thousand fresh troops.

In a last ditch try, Syracuse put herself in the Spartan's hands. It proved a wise decision. Before the end of summer, Gylippus completed a cross wall through a small opening in the Athenian fortifications and pushed his enemy down into a swampy bottom along the edge of the Great Harbor. Syracusan troops controlled Epipolae, and Nicias, bewildered by his unexpected reversals, was looking to his ships as a last chance of victory.

That winter the desperate Athenian general wrote home decrying the state of both his men and the ships and stating flatly that Athens must either recall the fleet completely or send another force in no way inferior to the first. Athens proudly refused to recall the expedition and began preparing another fleet under her best commander, Demosthenes, and another general, Eurymedon.

In the spring of 413 B.C., King Agis of Sparta, at the prodding of Alcibiades, established a permanent garrison at Decelea, about ten miles from Athens. Alcibiades had achieved an old dream—to renew the Peloponnesian War. But things were opposite the way he'd dreamed them. The fortification of Decelea hurled Athens into a two-front war, and wasted her resources. For the first time in eight years, refugees flocked into Athens from the countryside.

Even in the face of such precipitate danger the arrogant Athenians dismissed Demosthenes and his fleet to Sicily. While they were on the way, Nicias suffered his first naval defeat at the hands of the Syracusans.

Gylippus was preparing yet another sea offensive when Demosthenes arrived with seventy-three fighting galleys and went into action without delay. Knowing the possession of Epipolae was crucial to ultimate victory, he fashioned a daring nighttime attack against the Syracusan forts on its crest. After initial triumphs his troops became overconfident, fell into confusion, and slaughtered each other in the dark. Many Athenians panicked and threw themselves down from the precipices. Those who managed to reach the plain below were cut down by the Syracusan cavalry. Again the Athenians had failed utterly, and after another unfortunate month, Nicias belatedly ordered total evacuation.

The fleet prepared for withdrawal under absolute security, for if the enemy discovered that the besiegers were in fact besieged, he would write a quick and disastrous finale to an already fruitless expedition.

On the night of August 27, 413 B.C., a bright full moon lit the paths of dinghies secretly shuttling sailors to the ships. When the first light of morning stretched across the water, the prodigious fleet that now numbered over two hundred fighting ships would be fully manned, provisioned, and ready to sail for Attica. But for an untimely lunar eclipse the Athenians might have sneaked away.

In the brightest part of the night the horrible shadow crossed the moon. All semblance of silence disappeared among lamentations and prayers for deliverance. Demosthenes kept coaxing that the preparations continue, realizing the eclipse actually gave him the advantage of more secrecy. But his superstitious men rebelled. Soon afterward Nicias ordered him to disembark. Against Demosthenes' protests, Nicias insisted they remain where they were for thrice nine days as the soothsayers demanded.

The confusion in the night didn't escape Gylippus' observation, and the Spartan correctly reasoned that the Athenians were trying to escape. Without delay he ordered naval exercises, and within a few days his eager fleet rowed into the harbor, cut off the Athenian right, killed Eurymedon, and chased the confused Athenians to shore. Immediately the Syracusans sealed the mouth of the harbor with sunken ships. With the Athenians bottled in the confines of the harbor, lacking space to maneuver, the reinforced prows of the well-maintained Syracusan galleys would thereafter be devastating.

Thinking they were going home, the Athenians had sent messages to their allies halting further supply shipments. Facing starvation, they withdrew from their advanced positions to a walled enclave barely large enough for their remaining stores, their wounded, and those suffering from marsh sickness. Every able-bodied man, regardless of his function, then went aboard for a final attempt to force open the harbor.

Over two hundred Athenian and an equal number of Syracusan ships swarmed into the boiling harbor. The gnashing of hulls sounded for hours, observed in agony by the rival armies assembled along the shore. Depending on their vantage, soldiers cheered the sinking of an enemy ship or despaired when one of their own was overcome.

At last, after a courageous effort, the Athenian formations broke and, with a great cry, fled in open rout to shore. As defeated comrades scrambled up the bank, complete despair and panic settled over the Athenian enclave. The suffering troops lost their confidence and refused to go aboard anymore. They burnt their sixty remaining ships to keep them from falling to the enemy. Two days later they began a perilous march across the foreign countryside, hoping by some miracle to reach a friendly town. They left the dead behind unburied. The wounded and ill hobbled behind until they dropped under the hostile Sicilian sky.

Nicias marched ahead commanding a still formidable force of about forty thousand, while the forces of Demosthenes, numbering over ten thousand, brought up the rear. Gylippus understood their desperation and dared not confront them directly. Rather he stationed his darters and light infantry at a distance and sent a relentless rain of missiles that peeled the flesh from their outer ranks.

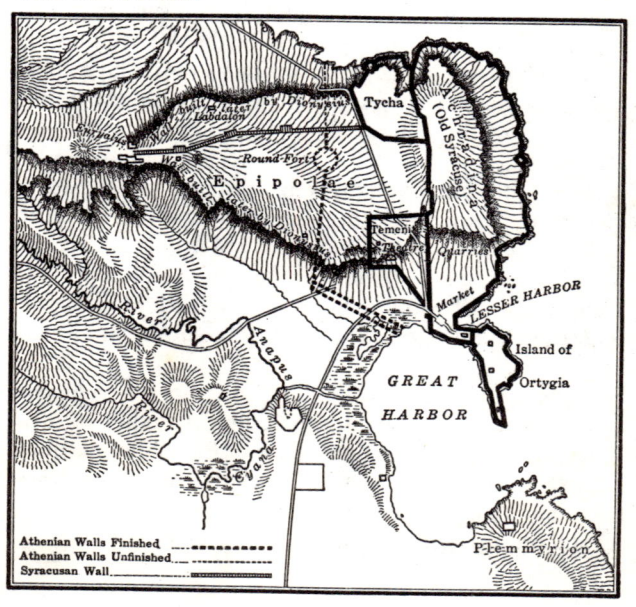

Plan of the Siege of Syracuse

The Spartan finally forced Demosthenes to halt his troops and draw them up for battle. The pause opened the distance between the Athenian forces and enabled Gylippus to surround Demosthenes. Realizing his entire force was about to be destroyed, he surrendered.

The larger army continued painfully, their stomachs distended from hunger and their throats cracked with thirst. Nicias encouraged them to a last hope, for ahead cascaded the river Assinarus which would mark the beginning of their freedom—if they could pass over. When the army spied the fast-flowing torrent all order broke within the ranks. They rushed headlong into the water, each vying for the honor of being first to reach the steep bank opposite. They languished in the water using it as a cool balm for their infected sores, and they groveled in the shadows, drinking greedily.

Nicias had lost control. Helplessly he watched the Syracusans line the far bank and cut off his escape. Then the enemy cavalry swept down on him from the rear and butchered the remnants of the Athenian expedition who, once so eager to go to war with Syracuse, had now forgotten war completely. As the Assinarus colored with the ebbing life of his men, Nicias surrendered.

The Athenian prisoners were confined in salt quarries adjacent to Syracuse, where they were given only half a pint of grain and a pint of water daily. After seventy days some of those who had survived starvation, exposure, and lack of sanitation were sold into slavery. The rest were left exposed to die. So ended the Sicilian Expedition.

Although the Sicilian fiasco didn't end the Peloponnesian War, its historical importance shouldn't be discounted. Had the democratic politics of Athens not veered against Alcibiades and had the Athenians been victorious, the fledgling city of Rome might have been swallowed up in a far-ranging Greek empire. Our heritage of law might have been Greek rather than Roman. The Spanish, French, Portuguese, and Rumanian languages might have sprung from Greek, not from provincial Latin. Our current political structures might reflect the subsidiary of the Greek city-states. But the tide of fate was running the other way. Athens was forced to forget the west and renew her efforts against Sparta.

When news of the holocaust reached Athens, his countrymen began to repent mistreating Alcibiades. However colorful and controversial he was, he was also their best hope of victory. In their blindness they'd driven him away and he'd made them pay bitterly. Now, with their fleet destroyed and Agis encamped only ten miles from their walls, they faced the Spartans once again. And what was perhaps even more discouraging, Alcibiades himself was arrayed against them. The comic playwright, Aristophanes, well expressed the people's feelings toward their errant general: "They love, and hate, and cannot do without him."

Athens determined to fight to the end. Summoning what remained of her imperial grandeur, she levied quotas for ship-building materials on her dominions. That winter the shipyards at Piraeus hummed with a fever, a precipitous race against time to outfit another fleet before the return of warm weather. Most of the city's remaining wealth was plunged into the enterprise, and by spring, the resilient democracy put to sea another fleet. She chose new generals and immediately sent them to restore her interests in the states that had revolted her alliance in her moment of weakness.

About the time the new fleet was putting forth, the Athenians received news that Alcibiades had taken command of the Spartan navy in Ionia, and that his transfer to that theater of the war was occasioned by a falling-out with Agis. The story infused Athens with new laughter. Despite his newly acquired Spartan

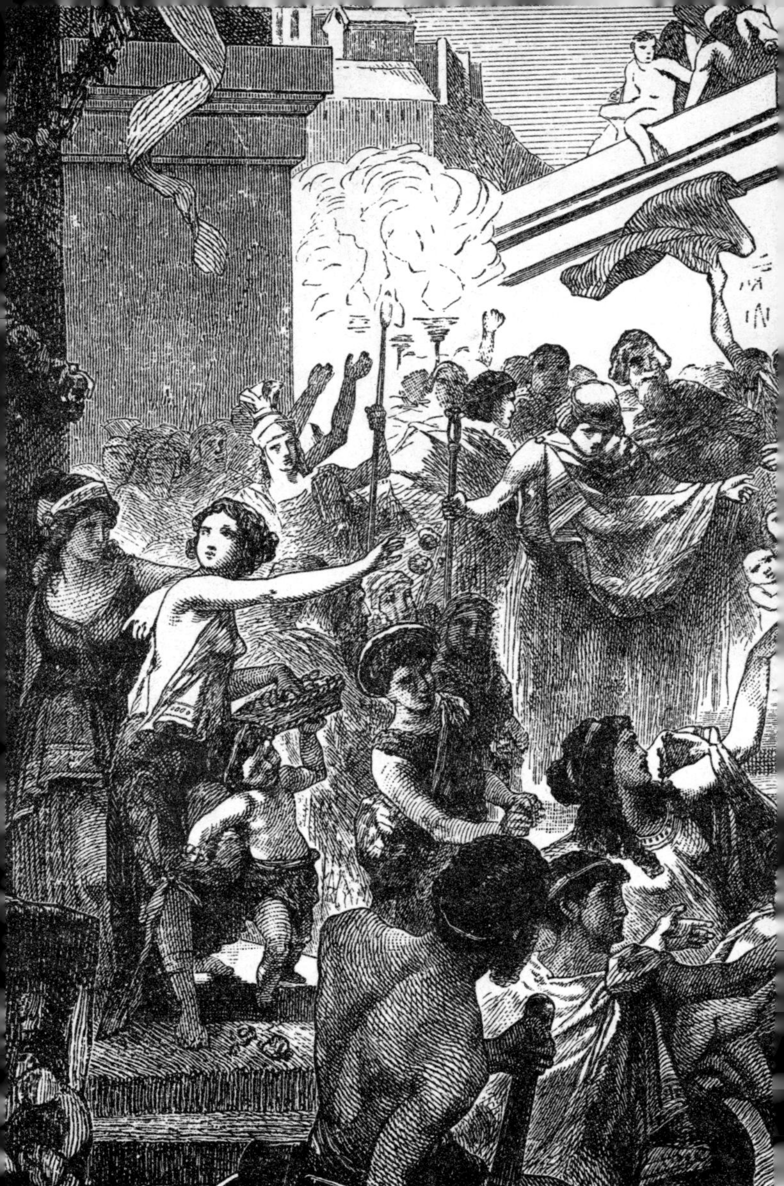

The return of Alcibiades to Athens

habits, the playboy of Athens was still himself. After encouraging Agis to fortify Decelea, Alcibiades had used his absence to corrupt the king's young wife, Timaea. He'd fathered a son by her and publicly proclaimed that he'd wished to father a line of Spartan kings! Agis was enraged, and grinning Alcibiades no longer dared set foot on the Peloponnese.

The year 412 B.C. began inauspiciously for Alcibiades. He'd betrayed the Athenians and angered the most powerful Spartan. His days in command of the Spartan fleet in Ionia were numbered. He seemed to have no place to go. There remained an alternative, however—the Persians. Both Greek belligerents were wooing Persian favor, knowing that Persian ships and money would quickly tip the balance of the war. Alcibiades offered his services to Tissaphernes, the King of Persia's satrap at Sardis, who accepted them enthusiastically.

Alcibiades became popular in the Persian's court by donning all the rich gowns and trappings of royalty—the same chameleon quality that had endeared him to the Spartans, but in reverse. Although Tissaphernes was under orders to supply both ships and money to Sparta, Alcibiades persuaded him to hold his support from either side and play an equalizing role while the Greek states wore themselves down. Both would then be easy conquests for the Persians.

As his days with Tissaphernes wore on, Alcibiades began to wish for his homeland. But would Athens receive him again? Aware that the veering fortunes of war had caused deep questioning of democratic government at Athens, he sent a message to the commanding generals at Samos where the new Athenian fleet was harbored. He informed them of his influence with the Persians and promised them Tissaphernes' support on one condition: They must overthrow democracy and establish an oligarchy friendly to him.

The proposal found favor with most of the generals,

and they hastened home to set off a revolution. By 411 B.C., Athens had an unpopular oligarchy supposedly enfranchising five thousand citizens, but which really centered power in the hands of four hundred leading men. Once the oligarchy had grasped power, however, they turned their backs on Alcibiades and prosecuted the war with little vigor hoping that the Spartans, who had always befriended government by the few, would give them favorable terms. Proponents of the war or of popular government were terrified into submission or executed.

The Samos-based fleet raged indignant at the turn of events in Athens and commanded Alcibiades to return as their general. In another incredible turnabout, Alcibiades became the champion of democracy within months after he'd been instrumental in its overthrow. Going to Samos he immediately proved his value by doing Athens two favors which saved her from total defeat by the Spartans:

First, he dissuaded the generals and men alike from sailing to Athens to drive out the oligarchy. He pointed out that civil war in Athens meant the revolt of the entire Delian League and certain conquest by the Lacedaemonians. Second, he sailed to meet Tissaphernes and persuaded him not to send the Phoenician fleet to the aid of Sparta as Cyrus, the younger son of the King of Persia, had commanded. Shortly afterward, the decisions of Alcibiades proved their consummate wisdom. The oligarchy at Athens was overthrown and his delighted countrymen commanded him to return home.

Alcibiades didn't want to return without restoring the damages he'd caused his country. Setting out from Samos he undertook a sweeping campaign in the Aegean that nearly drove the Spartans to capitulation and gained him a deserved reputation for invincibility. In the space of three years he gained decisive victories at Abydos, Bithynia, and Chalcedon. While sailing the Hellespont to raise money he took Selymbria. Finally he reconquered Athens' rebellious ally, Byzantium, after sharp fighting.

By 408 B.C. he'd established Athens' control of the sea and done what no Athenian had done before him: brought his city continuous victories by land. He'd driven the Spartans from the Hellespont, and the people back home were proclaiming him a hero. Now, with an illustrious string of achievements under his belt, Alcibiades was ready to go home.

He set sail with his entire fleet, towing a throng of cargo ships loaded with shields, weapons, money, and other spoils of war. He was tense as he sailed into the harbor at Piraeus. How would the people look on him after all these years? His ships dropped anchor but he didn't disembark. Let there first be some sign of affection. Then he saw his cousin Euryptolemos standing on the shore with a group of old friends. They were waving to him. Representatives of the Assembly rowed out in dinghies to welcome him ashore.

For the first time in seven years Alcibiades was home. He and his countrymen laughed and cried together and forgave each other their mutual betrayals. He chided them for their harsh decrees against his life and property and they eagerly restored him the estate they had confiscated years ago. Garlands showered down around his shoulders. People fought to touch his garments. They embraced him and gave him gifts. They publicly created him full general with absolute power and placed on his head a golden crown. Some even attempted to proclaim him king. A few watched with envy but they dared not act in the face of popular sentiment. Alcibiades had come. Things were right with the Athenians again.

Alcibiades stayed in Athens just long enough to give protection to the celebrants who marched to Eleusis to celebrate the holy mysteries—a religious practice that had been abandoned with the coming of Agis.

Then he sailed away again leaving the Athenians confident he would end the war shortly.

But what neither Alcibiades nor his countrymen understood was that Athens had fought too long a war. Money was running out, forcing the generals to spend much time seeking funds to pay their troops. To make matters worse, Sparta had sent out a new and talented commander named Lysander, who had persuaded Cyrus to free the money Tissaphernes was holding. Spartan troops now received four obols a day while the Athenians seldom received three. Many troops defected to the side promising higher pay, and it was the sheer force of Alcibiades' personality that was largely holding the Athenian navy together.

Under these circumstances Alcibiades needed to defeat Lysander quickly and decisively. He pursued the Spartan as far as Ephesus and there left Antioches, his second in command, with instructions not to engage in battle while he went into Ionia seeking funds. But Antioches disobeyed and sailed on the Spartan fleet. Lysander, striking back, put the Athenians to flight and seized several ships.

Back in Athens the old mistrust and animosity flared again. One of Alcibiades' generals returned to misrepresent him in hopes of advancing his own career in the army. The people had expected too much in believing Alcibiades invincible, especially with money running low. Now, in a moment of frustration, they dismissed him for the second time. The defeat of Antioches was a minor naval loss. In itself it meant little. But because it destroyed Alcibiades, it took on incredible importance. Alcibiades left the fleet and spent the next two years building his own mercenary army.

Athens spent the next two years chasing Lysander. Finally, in 405 B.C., Thydeus, Menander, and Adimantus, the new Athenian generals, brought the entire fleet of over two hundred ships ashore at Aegospotami, an

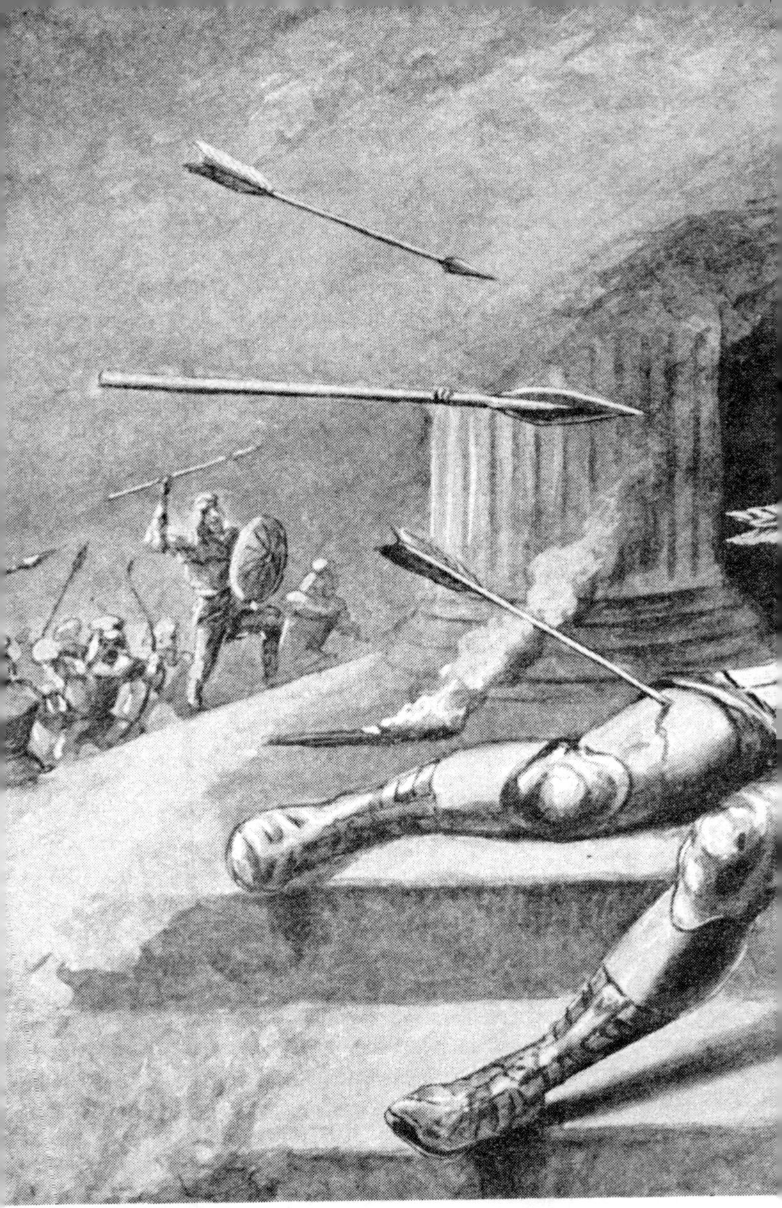

The death of Alcibiades

open beach some distance from Sestos. Not far off, Lysander was anchored at Lampsacus. The Athenians outnumbered Lysander, held him in contempt, and approached the battle carelessly. It became their daily custom to sail up to the Spartan fleet, challenge it to battle, be refused, and then return to Aegospotami where they would disembark and dismiss their men for the night.

Alcibiades wasn't far off and saw they were in mortal danger. Lysander, although lying back, was fully arming his ships each day and waiting for an opening. It was only a matter of time until he would fall upon the disorganized Athenians in their unfortified camp and demolish them. In desperation Alcibiades tried to warn the Athenian generals. Arriving in camp on horseback, he pleaded with them to remove the fleet to the harbor at Sestos where supplies would be easier to procure and where there was natural protection. He promised to attack Lampsacus with his band of Thracian mercenaries, and drive the Spartans onto the sea. But the Athenian generals laughed at Alcibiades and dismissed him. Pompously they boasted that they were now in command.

Only two days later the Athenians again sailed up to Lysander, challenged him, and sailed back to Aegospotami. They failed to notice the two observation ships that followed them.

The observation ships watched the Athenians disembark, then rowed quickly back to Lampsacus. Still some distance from the Spartan fleet, one of them raised a bronze shield in the afternoon sun. It was the signal for battle. Lysander raced to Aegospotami and fell on the empty Athenian fleet, destroying it entirely. He put three thousand Athenian captives to the sword. For the second time Athens had turned her back on Alcibiades and lost her fleet. She never got a chance to do it again.

THE RISE OF ALCIBIADES

Lysander sailed to Athens and within a year took the city by siege. The Spartans began installing oligarchies in all the former Athenian colonies and inflicted a government of thirty tyrants (to the Athenians, the word "tyrant" simply meant "absolute ruler") on Athens herself. Athens, by tradition democratic, chafed under the tyrants. Again she repented her mistrust of Alcibiades, and in her extremity she entertained the myth that he would someday return to free her. Lysander realized he could never control Athens while the citizens entertained their hopes in Alcibiades. He sent execution orders to Phrygia where the Athenian general was living with his mistress, Timandra.

On a tragic day in 404 B.C., the house of Alcibiades burst into flame. Grasping his sword and wrapping his cloak about his left arm to ward off the flame, Alcibiades struggled through the hot smoke into the courtyard. From a distance, assassins rained darts on him and hacked him to pieces. There is a story that Timandra cradled his bleeding head in her lap and that she cried as she buried him.

Such was the end of Alcibiades, and so ended the hope of the Greek state that had risen to challenge the unsurpassable power of Sparta. Neither Athens nor Alcibiades could survive the mercurial course run by democracy under the pressure of twenty-seven years of war, and certainly no man and no state ever more profoundly exemplified the axiom: "Things do not just happen; they are *made* to happen." Yet neither Athens nor Alcibiades would have caused the results that occurred could they have foreseen them. The tragic poet Euripides summarized the parallel fates of Athens and Alcibiades in the closing lines of his immortal *Andromache:*

> Past our telling the ways of heaven,
> The gods accomplish the unforeseen.
> What all awaited, fails of achievement;
> God arranges what none could dream.

Dessiné d'après un Hermès trouvé à Tivoli, et Gravé par Ambroise Tardieu.

Alexander the Great

THE AGE OF ALEXANDER

By Ronald Leal

*H*e was destined to pass as a conqueror across all the known world and, to most of the peoples of that world, he became a god in his own lifetime. Blond, boyish, beardless, and small by today's standards, this living god was doomed to die at the age of 33, but before his death he was to overwhelm lands that would stretch from New York to Los Angeles and beyond, from Maine to Sonora, Mexico.

From Macedonia and Greece he would extend his domain to include all or part of present-day Turkey, Syria, Lebanon, Israel, Jordan, Egypt, Libya, Cyprus, Soviet Central Asia, Iran, Iraq, Afghanistan, and Pakistan. And he so captured the imagination of the people he conquered that he was more often hailed as a liberator than a conqueror. His conquests opened the way for an eastward diffusion of Greek trade, art, and thought and, in turn, Babylonian science, Persian gold, and the new idea of power politics devised by the Macedonians in their newly taken lands were brought east to make a lasting influence on the Greeks.

Alexander III, of Macedonia, who was to become known as Alexander the Great (the use of the surname is proven as far back as the first century B.C.), was born of the union between King Philip II of Macedonia and Olympias, the orphaned daughter of the monarch of the mountain kingdom of Spirus, which lay near present day Albania.

A fiery, passionate woman who, along with her brother, had been shouldered aside after the death of her father by a scheming uncle, Olympias met Philip in 357 B.C. when they both were being initiated into the mysteries of rites of Kabirioi (a mother earth deity, the details of the worship have been lost) on the island of Samothrace off the Thracian shore in the North Aegean Sea.

The beauty of the Epirote princess was sufficient to attract Philip and, too, politician that he was, he possibly entertained thoughts of obtaining an interest in the throne of Spirus—or at least making a valuable ally of the mountain kingdom. Olympias, who claimed to be descended from the Greek warrior Achilles (and would instill in her son such admiration for the latter that it would become all consuming and life lasting), returned Philip's glances with like ardor, we are told by the ancient historians. Not only did he marry her but he named her his queen, overlooking any claims that his four previous wives might have had to the throne.

Something of a mystic and deeply religious, Olympias had barely been established in court at Pella, the capital of Macedonia, when her excesses, her outbursts of violent temperament, and certain other aspects of her er-

Philip II of Macedonia

ratic personality became the talk of the kingdom. The fact that she kept great tame serpents in her room and her public disapproval of Philip's ever wandering eye coupled with her domineering nature were, no doubt, the reasons Philip's ardor rapidly cooled.

Not only was Olympias strange and terrible, but she was a visionary, she claimed—and probably a very evil one at that. Soon after Alexander's birth in midsummer of 356 B.C. (some authorities ascertain that Alexander was born in October but the Macedonians moved the time of his birth back to midsummer in order that history might record that Philip received three glorious messages simultaneously—that Parmenio, his chief general, had conquered the Illyrians in a great battle; that his race horse had won a victory at the Olympic games; and that Alexander III had been born at Pella), she almost convinced Philip that he was not the father of the child at all but that the god Zeus had visited her in her bedchamber and fathered the infant. Zeus had mystic powers of fertility and manifested his presence in shooting stars and thunderbolts and, according to Olympias, at least once in the form of a snake.

In his early childhood Alexander was almost entirely under the influence of Olympias and his nurse, Lanice, for reasons of state that we will get to shortly. Olympias instilled in her child a fascination with magic and taught him, at an early age, to perform mystic rites. It would seem that she was determined to make her son as unlike Philip as possible as she had grown to hate the king with a grand passion.

Olympias lavished affection on the young prince but, in her erratic manner, counteracted it by placing him under tutelage of an Epirote relative named Leonidas, who was so stern in his discipline of the boy that he would not allow Alexander to eat the rich food served at the palace table—although Olympias and Lanice

Olympias

often smuggled sweets to the youth to fortify him against the meager meals allowed by Leonidas. In later years, according to Plutarch, Alexander would recall that his tutor provided him with the best possible diet —"a night march to prepare for breakfast and a moderate breakfast to create an appetite for supper."

But Leonidas is credited with curbing Alexander's instinctive quick temper and trained him to become an exceptional swordsman and athlete—excellent at running, hunting, riding, and in all competitive games, which he held in contempt.

Meanwhile Olympias continued to vent her personal vendetta toward Philip. She let neither her religious peculiarities nor her continuing active interest in the affairs of Epirus interfere with her efforts to alienate young Alexander from his father. And for the first few years of Alexander's life she had her way, for Philip, by war and diplomacy, was much too occupied at raising Macedonia to the headship of the Greek states to concern himself with his queen's intrigues.

When Philip became regent of Macedonia early in 359 B.C., at the age of 23, his country stood in somewhat of an ambiguous relationship with the rest of the Greek world. Philip, like his predecessors on the Macedonian throne, was of Greek descent and, also like them, he cast an envious eye to the south and the more culturally advanced city-states of Athens and Thebes.

While the Macedonians considered themselves one people and, as such, were the first nation, Athens, Thebes, and the other Greek city-states considered them semi-barbarians at best. The Macedonians had contributed virtually nothing to Greek culture and had proved themselves unworthy of even being called Hellenic by fighting against the Greeks in the Persian wars. But Philip was something of a practical genius, both on the battlefield and at the diplomatic table.

He had considerable experience behind him when he became regent—as a hostage at Thebes he had consorted with Epaminondas and formed a most lively admiration for him; he had then governed a province of Macedonia to his credit. And, while his private life was somewhat dissolute and his adversaries had every reason in the world to chide him for his immoderate love of wine and women, they could but admire his political gifts.

As soon as he became regent Philip set about tidying up the very loose ship that was Macedonia with the explicit idea of raising her to the leadership of the disunited Greek states—and with the ultimate aim of the complete subjugation of all of Greece. As a hostage at Thebes, Philip had learned much of Greek military tactics, strategy, and intrigue. Putting his knowledge to practical use, he quickly expanded at the expense of all his neighbors.

He conquered two provinces from Epirus, seized Amphipolis and Pydna by tricking the Athenians in a series of cunning negotiations, and annexed the gold-bearing district of Mount Pangaeum from Thrace, which Athens had long claimed but had been unsuccessful in holding because she was unable to control the irrational raids of the half-wild Thracian chieftains. The Athenians actually backed Philip in his campaign against Thrace, intending to use the Macedonians as dupes to stabilize the back country to their benefit.

But the Athenians were the dupes, as they learned when Philip claimed the city of Amphipolis and the nearby gold mines for Macedonia. The gold mines yielded him 1,000 talents of gold yearly—the equivalent of eight million dollars today. With his new riches the Macedonian king created an army that made him the foremost military commander of his time. Philip's professional army, trained to fight in a new phalanx formation—a solid yet flexible body of men, marching in close order, sometimes 16 ranks deep, and armed with spears from 16 to 23 feet long.

Turning his attention to the north, Philip drove back the Paeonian and Illyrian barbarians and pursued a policy of internal colonization in recently conquered territories which resulted in the exploitation and Hellenization of regions which had on the whole remained very barbarous until his time. He also used his newfound wealth to secure the services of Greek poets and artists who frequented his court in large numbers and adorned Pella with many beautiful buildings.

And all the while he was putting his own house in order, Philip encouraged dissension among the Greek states — hence, while they fought each other, he increased his forces and added to his domains either by military force or by alliances in marriage. "Taken all in," concluded a contemporary, "Europe has not yet produced such a man as Philip, son of Amyntas."

Philip's advance in the first ten years of his reign was relatively easy because Athens, the only Greek city-state strong enough to oppose him, chose to ignore him. The Athenians were more interested in their material advantage and artistic achievement than the conquests of the "northern barbarians." Athens no longer had faith in its destiny; its rich were happy to be freed from the crushing weight of war contributions and the common people basked in prosperity with no risks attached. Their ennui was such that Philip's seizure of Methone—the only place that Athens still occupied on the Macedonian coast—in 354 stirred not a ripple of opposition. And, too, Philip had won supporters, even in Athens.

Methodically Philip pursued the execution of his plans to rule over all the Greek states. Without neglecting his unruly barbarian neighbors, he turned the main body of his army toward the Greek cities on the coast. In 348 he seized and destroyed Olynthus and, if anything, gained additional support in Athens. The orator

Isocrates, in 346, appealed to Philip to unite the Greeks and take the offensive against Persia. But Isocrates was opposed by the master of Greek oratory, Demosthenes, who appealed to his countrymen to resist the "tyrant" Philip, who "blusters and talks big, [who] cannot rest content with what he has conquered, he is always taking in more, everywhere he is casting his net around us, we sit and do nothing . . ."

But before he completed the conquest of Greece, Philip turned his attention to more personal matters. He summoned Aristotle (in 343) to the capital to direct the education of his 13-year-old son and heir-apparent, Alexander. For three years Aristotle tutored the boy and some of his companions—"suitable companions" chosen by Philip at Mieza, near Pella. During these formative years Alexander's keen mind became thoroughly Greek in character, while his romantic imagination was spurred by Homer and his supposed ancestors, Heracles and Achilles.

Under Aristotle's tutorage he was taught letters, grammar, rhetoric, and dialectic; arithmetic, geometry, and astronomy. The master instilled in the pupil such a love for the writings of Homer that, on his expedition to Asia, Alexander took along a text of the *Iliad,* which Aristotle had edited for him, and kept it with his dagger under his pillow at night. In the three years that he taught Alexander, Aristotle implanted in the youth a love of learning of encyclopedic scope, but the prince was no slavish imitator of his tutor and was known to take exception to some of his public pronouncements.

His mysticism tempered by learning, and thoroughly prepared by his father to conquer, Alexander now dreamed of glory. Whenever he heard of another of Philip's victories, he lamented, "Will my father leave me nothing to do?"

But there was plenty left for Alexander to do and, at the age of 16, he was ready to enter the arena of history. His father placed the young prince in the army where he learned the techniques of warfare, for which he quickly demonstrated a remarkable aptitude. During one of Philip's many absences from Macedonia, Alexander—still in his 16th year—commanded and repelled a rising of the hill tribes on the northern border, all the while efficiently governing the state in his father's absence. Two years later he rejoined Philip's army just before the battle of Chaeronea.

In 338 B.C. Philip led his army into the heart of Greece to a plain near the village of Chaeronea, in Boeotia, to meet the combined armies of Athens and Thebes, with their allies from nearby Thessaly. Not only did Philip easily rout the allied force, but Alexander, mounted on his black charger Bucepalus, led the charge that crashed the Theban wing. Then, turning, he caught the Sacred Band of Thebes, who had sworn to die fighting rather than surrender, between his forces and those of Philip. With Philip on the right and Alexander on the left, all 300 members of the Sacred Band died fighting and their Greek allies were annihilated.

It was a decisive victory, one that elevated Philip finally to mastery of all the Greek city-states—with the exception of Sparta. Soon after Chaeronea, Philip called together at Corinth representatives of most of the states in Greece and joined them in the federation known as the League of Corinth. Philip, of course, was appointed commander in chief of the League and immediately planned a war of revenge against Persia—to punish her for the Persian invasion of Greece a century and a half earlier. It is doubtful that Philip seriously intended to conquer Persia, a rich and mighty state, well governed and able to dispose large armies of disciplined, courageous men. Persia stretched 2,700 miles from the Hellespoint (Dardanelles) across Asia Minor through Syria, Palestine, and Egypt, and then eastward through Mesopotamia and Iran to India.

Demosthenes practicing oratory

With the formation of the League of Corinth Philip had achieved what theretofore had scarcely been thought possible—he had united Greece. The only door open to his gaining further glory was the planned invasion of Persia. But unfortunately—for Philip—he delayed his departure two years, during which time he alternately attended to state business, planned the Persian campaign, and gave vent to his weakness for wine, women, and song.

In 337 Philip finally repudiated Olympias as his queen in favor of his new wife, a Macedonian named Cleopatra. According to Plutarch, Alexander sat in grim silence at his father's wedding while the other guests, adhering to custom, drank themselves into a stupor.

When Attalus, the uncle of the 16-year-old bride, proposed a toast to the as yet unborn child of Philip and Cleopatra, and called upon the guests to pray to the gods for a "legitimate heir to the throne" of Macedonia, he suggested that, as Cleopatra was Macedonian and her child would be without the foreign Epirote strain Alexander had inherited from Olympias, the child would be the lawful successor of Philip. Alexander, enraged, sprang to his feet and hurled his wine cup at Attalus, who ducked and threw his own cup at Alexander.

In the pandemonium that followed, Philip staggered to his feet and threw himself at Alexander, his sword drawn, apparently determined to kill the young prince. Blind drunk, Philip fell on his face, whereupon Alexander pointed at his father and cried out scornfully that there was a man preparing to pass from Europe to Asia who could not pass from one chair to another. Then he left the hall and that night he and Olympias left Pella for Epirus.

The breach in the house of Philip was patched, if uneasily so, by Demaratus of Corinth who admonished Philip for his concern with Greek unity when his own house was torn by "so many dissensions and calamities." Philip, won over by the logic of Demaratus, sent for Alexander, who reluctantly returned to the Macedonian capital. And Olympias returned to Pella with him.

Olympias, of course, was incensed when Cleopatra did give birth to a son. According to Plutarch, when Olympias learned that a *hetairos* named Pausanias bore a grudge against Philip, she "encouraged and exasperated the enraged youth to revenge," and he made plans to murder the king. Whether Alexander was aware of the assassination plot (if there was one) is not known, but it is certain that his star at the Macedonian court was on the wane.

In July of 336 B.C., in the midst of celebrating the marriage of his daughter (Alexander's sister) to her uncle Alexander I, of Epirus, Philip was stabbed by Pausanias (who may have been a Persian agent) before a great concourse from all the Greek world. At the age of 20, Alexander fell heir to Philip's kingdom, his army, his plan of the Asiatic expedition, and the command of the League of Corinth.

In one respect Alexander was false to the teachings of Aristotle—because he had been taught by Leonidas and his mother to believe that he was a superman, he behaved like one. Where Philip had been cautious, patient, and often devious—and thought out his plan of action thoroughly before acting on it—Alexander was headstrong and liked to settle problems by immediate action. In making decisions with great speed, he took extraordinary risks, his sheer force and drive overcoming all odds. But he, too, had his cautious streak.

Before setting out for Asia, he spent the two years after Philip's death extending his dominions northward to the Danube River and westward to the Adriatic Sea. Then he turned his attention to Greece, where Thebes and Athens were threatening to bolt the Corinth League.

69

He put down the insurrection in Thebes in 335 B.C. in a lightning campaign that dried up all hopes of revolt and freedom from Macedonian rule raised by Philip's death. To show his implacable resolution, he razed Thebes to the ground except for the temples and the poet Pindar's house. However, as Philip had been after the battle of Chaeronea, he was generous to Athens. Then, less than two years after his ascension to the throne—having secured it by liquidating all the pretenders—he mobilized the Macedonian army and the Hellenic league contingents and departed for Asia.

The expedition to Asia, when at last it was ready to set out, had an air of permanence about it. His entourage sometimes numbered 120,000 and included artists, poets, philosophers, and historians. There were also surveyors and engineers to build battle equipment, geographers to map captured territories, architects to lay out new cities, hydrographers, geologists, botanists, and other scientists to study the phenomena of Asia, and amid the host trudged traders, opportunists, and the women and children of his soldiers.

Among the officers was Aristotle's nephew, Callisthenes, the historian who had studied with Alexander in Mieza. In central Asia, Callisthenes would be implicated in a plot to murder Alexander, arrested and executed. Aristotle so hated Alexander for what he considered the murder of Callisthenes—and so powerful was his influence among the poets and historians of Greece—that when the generation that knew Alexander personally died out, there was not one favorable biography of the conqueror written for three centuries. It was due to the far-reaching influence of Aristotle that all the early biographies depicted Alexander as a cunning, blood-thirsty and fantastically lucky despot. Also worth noting among the officers that left Pella with Alexander was "the gentle Hephaestion," Alexander's confidant and friend who would serve faithfully at the side of his king until his death in 324 B.C.

Alexander left Pella in the spring of 334 B.C., leading his 30,000 foot soldiers and 5,000 cavalry. He crossed the Axios River with the reckless confidence of a man who knew that he could not fail. He was never to return to Macedonia.

Alexander's invasion of Persia was, at best, a reckless undertaking—at least on the surface. True, Persia was ruled by Darius III, a cruel despot and anything but a brave man. A descendant of the great Persian kings of the Achaemenid Dynasty—Cyrus the Great, Darius I, and Xerxes—Darius III lacked all of the sterling qualities of his forebearers and, in fact, had come to the throne in June of 336 through the murder of his predecessor, Areses. But while Darius ruled, Persia was actually governed by a patriotic and devoted military caste that was only too eager to show its prowess in a war against the Greeks. The Persians were rich both in money and men and their army included a force of Greek mercenaries comparable to Alexander's own soldiers.

Alexander covered the 300 miles from Pella to the Dardanelles in 20 days and bivouacked at Sestos on the western shore. From a ridge above Sestos, he looked across the straits of the Hellespont to the western reaches of the Persian Empire. And, as Alexander's troops boarded the galleys that would carry them to the eastern shore, the Persians were hastily assembling an army at the Granicus River two days' march inland.

Alexander left the ferrying of his troops to his general, Parmenion. Taking the helm of a galley himself, he steered south to Troy where he went through the dramatic acts of sacrifice to the Ilian Athena to obtain a potent symbol of good luck. Then he anointed and crowned with garlands the tomb of his mythical ancestor, Achilles. Sacred armor from the Trojan War, legend tells us, lay in Troy's temple of Athena. Exchanging pieces of his own armor for the shield of Achilles that eight years later was to save his life near the Indus, Alexander marched to his first meeting with the Persians.

Darius III considered it beneath his dignity to bother personally with the young upstart from Greece. He left that matter up to his satraps in Asia Minor. Alexander found the Persian army spread along the Granicus (now the Kocabas) near the present town of Biga. Leading his army in a lightning strike across the river into the center of the Persian force, Alexander saw the answer to his prayers to Athena appear before his eyes. The Persians broke in disorder and fled.

Alexander had won his first decisive victory. He ordered the Macedonian dead buried with honors and their families exempted from taxes and military conscription. Walking about the camp at night with Hephaestion at his side, he chatted with the wounded, encouraging each to brag of his deeds, further strengthening the increasing loyalty of his men. From the spoils of the victory, he sent 300 suits of Persian armor back to Athens. With them went the message, "Alexander, the son of Philip, and the Greeks, except the Spartans [Sparta had refused to join the League of Corinth], have won this spoil from the barbarians of Asia," hence expressing his contempt for the Persians as well as for the Spartans, whom he considered traitors.

With a firm foothold in Asia—and with the main body of the Persian army still more than 1,000 miles to the east and posing no immediate threat—he went about collecting an army that numbered perhaps 100,000 men. With the easy victory at the Granicus, Alexander's plan expanded. Originally his purpose had been to destroy the Persian army—now he would take over the entire Persian Empire.

But before he could do that he had to destroy the Persian fleet, which, numerically superior to the Greek navy, controlled the seas. He turned south toward the Turkish coast to begin breaking the Persian hold on the Mediterranean by taking its maritime provinces, which were ripe for the plucking as they had originally been established by Greek immigrants.

At the end of seven months almost all of Asia Minor was his—he seized Sardes, then Ephesus, where the people stoned the Persian officials at Alexander's approach and welcomed the Macedonians. Alexander spread the word that he came as a liberator, not as a conqueror, and city after city opened its gates to him. He took Miletus by storm and restored democratic government and remitted taxes. When asked why he did not reap more tribute from so rich a conquest, Alexander replied, "I hate the gardener who cuts to the root the vegetables of which he ought to cull the leaves."

Next he marched on Halicarnassus, where a large Persian garrison held out, but the Macedonians stormed the town. The defeats of Phaselis, Perga, Aspendus, and Side followed.

Spring found Alexander marching to Gordium where only a few mounds and crumbled walls marked the site where fabled King Midas once held court. Here—according to legend—Alexander solved the puzzle of the famous Gordian knot by severing it with one stroke of his sword. Since legend held that whoever undid the knot would be the lord of Asia, Alexander added another omen to his favor.

From Gordium Alexander's army marched northeast to Ancyra (now Ankara, capital of Turkey) then southeast across the Anatolian Plateau to Tyana, through a pass in the Taurus Mountains called the Cilician Gates. All of Asia Minor was now successfully behind him. He knew that Darius III and his vast army were camped somewhere in the broad Syrian Plain and he feigned illness, hoping to entice Darius into the narrow plain of Cilicia. His intelligence service broke down for the first and only time as he got tired of waiting for Darius to come to him, so he crossed the Amanus Mountains in search of Darius. That same night, Darius crossed the mountains through a different pass in search of him.

In the morning Alexander found himself with Darius between him and home and his line of communications cut. He immediately retraced his route through the mountains and confronted Darius at Issus. It was the autumn of 333 B.C. There on the narrow plain beside the sea, the smaller Macedonian army met the larger Persian force. Alexander, leading his elite cavalry called the Companions, charged the Persian horsemen, the enemy front collapsed and Alexander raced toward the Persian king, who turned and fled the field and, despite rapid pursuit, managed to escape.

Returning to camp that night, he found that his men had chosen the tent of Darius for him, which was overflowing with oriental splendor. According to Plutarch, Alexander took off his armor and went to his bath, saying, "Let us go and wash off the sweat of battle in the bath of Darius." "No," said a Companion, "but rather in the bath of Alexander." Upon seeing the basins and pitchers and tubs and caskets, all of beautifully wrought gold, he remarked, "This, it would seem, is to be king." But for all the spoils he had taken, he kept for himself only a jeweled casket in which to carry his treasured *Iliad*. Plutarch says that he sent much of the treasure home to Olympias.

That night as Alexander was going to supper, one of the Companions told him that among the prisoners were the mother, wife, and two unmarried daughters of Darius, whom they believed to be dead. He sent word that Darius was alive and that they need have no fear of Alexander, for it was not upon them but upon Darius that he was waging war.

Another version of the story has it that on the following day Alexander, accompanied by his friend He-

Alexander training Bucephalus

phaestion, visited Darius' mother. She was in doubt which of them was Alexander, as they were dressed identically, and went to Hephaestion, who was the taller of the two, prostrating herself before him. When Hephaestion drew back and one of the attendants pointed out Alexander, saying he was the king, she was so ashamed of her mistake that she wanted to withdraw. But Alexander told her she had made no mistake, for Hephaestion was also Alexander.

This chivalrous courtesy which he supposedly showed Darius' women was a favorite theme for later rhetoricians and has been the subject of several paintings.

Actually it is doubted that Alexander ever saw either Darius' mother or his wife, who was reputedly the most beautiful woman in Asia. Later in a letter to Parmenion he wrote that he had not as much as seen the wife of Darius or desired to see her.

Darius sent a message that he wanted to negotiate and offered a ransom for his family but Alexander arrogantly replied that he must first surrender. Alexander's humane treatment of all captives greatly aided his cause and his chivalrous treatment of all captive women has been the cause of much speculation—as such was considered a sign of weakness in his time. Seeing that the Persian women were surpassingly stately and beautiful, he is supposed to merely have said in jest that "Persian women were torments to the eyes." According to the Royal Journal, the "official" truth was that Alexander never had a mistress and married only for political reasons. And, according to Plutarch, "Alexander sought no intimacy with any of them [the Persian women], nor indeed with any other women before marriage, except Barsine, who was taken prisoner at Damascus."

When Darius retired to the east to lick his wounds and reorganize his army, Alexander, instead of giving pursuit as the Persian king probably expected, turned south—and again gave his attention to the Persian fleet and maritime provinces of Lebanon, Israel, and Egypt. As he traveled south, between the mountains and the Mediterranean, his first objective was the city of Tyre in Lebanon. Tyre was a key naval base and the commercial center of the Middle East. Arriving there in January, 332 B.C., he found Tyre a proud, heavily fortified island city half a mile offshore. But, unlike the inhabitants of Ephesus and other coastal cities who had opened their gates to Alexander, had given him a hero's welcome, the people of Tyre resisted—and strongly.

Alexander ordered a 200-foot-wide mole built to the island for the use of his invading land troops, then built his own fleet to repel any aid of Tyre that might come from the sea. For seven months Alexander's Macedonians labored on the causeway and for seven months the people of Tyre resisted, raining stones and arrows down on the troops.

It was during that time that Alexander received a message from Darius, suing for peace. Darius offered Alexander the hand of his daughter in marriage, 10,000 talents of gold, and all the territory west of the Euphrates—one third of the Persian Empire.

When told of the offer, Parmenion said, "Were I Alexander, I would accept." And Alexander replied, "So would I, were I Parmenion." By refusing to bargain with Darius, Alexander gave definite evidence as to the reach of his designs. He would not be satisfied with part of Darius' Empire—he would take the whole.

At last Alexander's catapults were positioned within range of Tyre's east wall and shipborne battering rams hammered at the south wall. Tyre was defeated and the Persian fleet, left without a port, also fell to Alexander. Alexander totally destroyed Tyre and had the Tyrian people scattered to the winds, selling 30,000 of

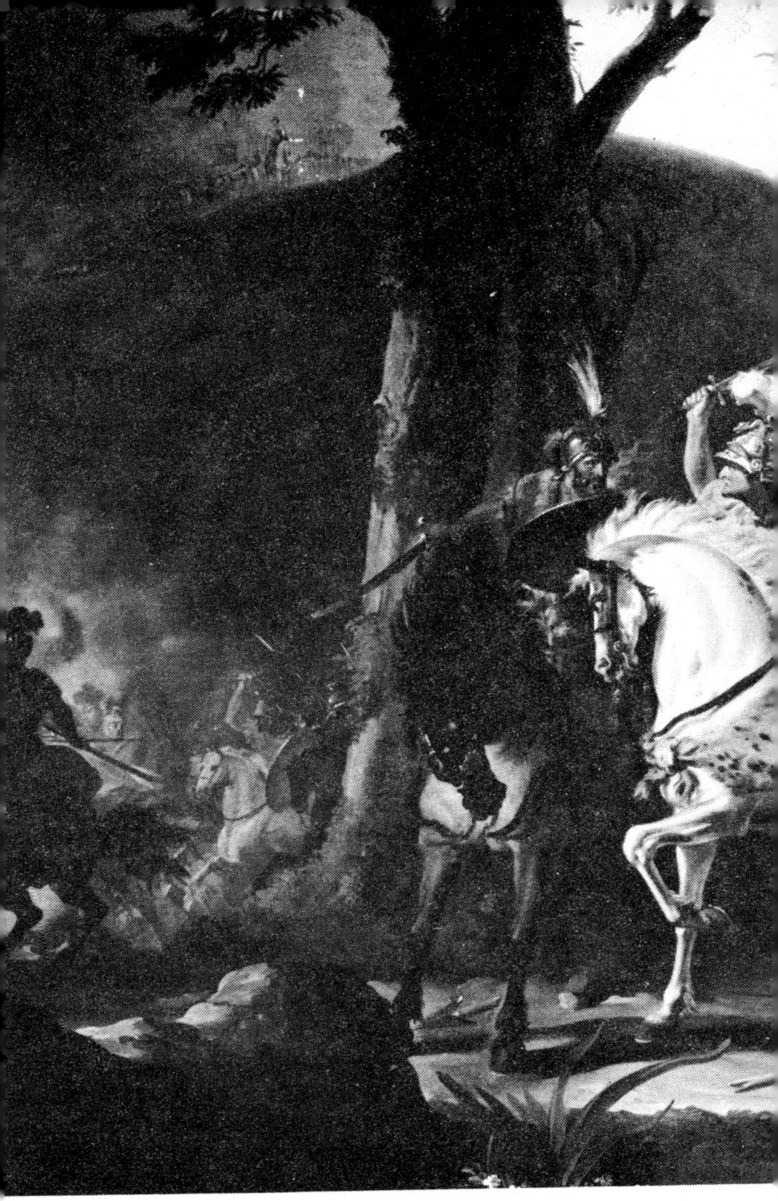

Alexander at the Battle of Granicus

them as slaves. Later historians would damn Alexander for his treatment of Tyre. On the other hand, the destruction of captured cities and the enslavement of their population was common practice in his time.

Gaza also offered a heroic resistance to the Macedonians which lasted two months but it fell and the population was dispersed. The way was now open for the conquest of Egypt.

The Egyptians hated the tyrannical Persian rule and welcomed Alexander as a deliverer. Not only did they welcome him with open arms, they were ready to crown him Pharaoh. He sacrificed piously to the gods of Memphis and planned a great city, Alexandria, at the Canopic mouth of the Nile. The first of 70-odd cities Alexander founded on his march, Alexandria was destined to be an administrative center for the eastern Mediterranean world which Alexander had now taken into his possession. Not only was the city to act as a link between East and West, its founding was essential to provide a commercial substitute for the destroyed Tyre. The site chosen for the city was on the west side of the western-most mouth of the Nile and, due to the currents of the Mediterranean, free from the river's silt.

According to Arrian, the second century A.D. historian, whose account of Alexander was drawn from the most authoritative contemporary sources, while the king was laying out the city in the winter of 332-331 B.C., "an overmastering desire came upon [Alexander]" to pay a visit to Zeus Ammon, the famous Oracle at Siwa Oasis in the Libyan Desert 300 miles to the southwest. While it is true that Zeus Ammon was second in importance only to Delphi in the eyes of the Greeks, Alexander's purpose in visiting Siwa Oasis was not entirely religious. No doubt he was determined to make sure the Libyan—or Western—Desert actually existed and would serve as a natural boundary for western reaches of his empire.

It took Alexander several weeks to reach the oasis and upon his arrival he was greeted by the chief priest of Ammon as the "son of Ammon." According to Arrian, Alexander then received "the answer his soul desired." He never disclosed that answer, but word soon spread that he had been told he would rule all lands. Then, turning to the practical purpose of his visit, Alexander bribed the priests to police the desert for him and accepted the surrender of envoys from Cyrene to the west.

In the spring of 331 B.C., Alexander left the Mediterranean, intent on finding Darius and destroying him and his army. He first returned to Tyre, where he rested his troops and made final arrangements for the administration of the conquered provinces. Then he marched swiftly northeast to the Tigris River to strike at the very heart of the Persian Empire. Marching his army swiftly northeast, he traversed Mesopotamia and crossed the Tigris on the day of a lunar eclipse—the 20th of September, 331 B.C.

In a broad plain near the village of Gaugamela, Alexander came face to face with the Persian army. Having found Darius' army, Alexander was now faced with the most serious problem which had yet confronted him for, since his defeat at Issus, the Persian king had gathered an immense armament which was said to rival in size that of his illustrious ancestor Xerxes who had invaded Greece 150 years before.

While it was unlikely that the Persian army did approach in size that which would be reported in later legend—a million infantry, 40,000 cavalry, 200 scythed chariots, and 15 elephants—it was much larger than Alexander's army and it extended so far beyond his flanks that it threatened to overlap his wings. While disadvantaged in size, the Greeks did possess two advantages: Darius' fear and the military genius of Alexander.

Fearing a surprise attack, Darius kept his army under arms the entire night before the battle. Not only did the lack of rest greatly reduce the vitality of the Persians but the rumors that spread like fire through the ranks that the Greeks were about to attack at any moment kept the Persians on edge and added to their natural fear.

Indeed, Alexander's general, Parmenion, seeing the plain before the Greek army lighted up with fires and hearing the sound of voices arising from the enemy camp, was so astonished at the size of the Persian army that he sought out Alexander and argued that it would be difficult to defeat such an army in the light of day and suggested that Alexander make a surprise night attack on the Persians. In answer Alexander gave his celebrated reply: "I will not steal my victory."

Rather than entertain thoughts of surprising the Persians at night, Alexander ordered his troops to take dinner and rest themselves well in preparation for the morning battle. And while his army slept he passed the night in front of his tent with his seer Aristander, celebrating mysterious sacred rites and making sacrifices. And no doubt forming the plan of battle that would rout the Persian army and destroy the Empire of Darius.

Alexander devised a rather simple plan of battle to meet the formidable bulk of the Persian army. He placed behind each wing a second line, which could resist an attack on either flank by the overlapping Persian line. And so, on the morning of October 1 of 331 B.C., the two armies lined up for battle.

Alexander's attack began with a cavalry charge toward the enemy's left; this he suddenly changed and directed the charge in the form of a wedge against the center where Darius himself was urging the Persian troops on to battle. No doubt Alexander had anticipated the next move of the cowardly King Darius—

Alexander the Great before Tyre

which was to turn and flee the field.

With their king retreating at full speed, the Persian army became completely demoralized. The remainder of Alexander's troops, lead by Parmenion, pressed forward and gained a complete victory. The battle at Gaugamela—usually called the battle of Arbela after the nearby town of that name—sealed the doom of the Persian Empire. Darius fled eastward into Media, but again Alexander, instead of giving chase after the Persian king, turned south. He would secure the southern provinces before dealing with Darius.

Leaving the stench rising from the dead at Gaugamela behind him, Alexander led his army south, following the Tigris into Babylon. As the Macedonian army approached the city about which the Greeks so often spoke but knew little, a procession of priests and people came streaming through the gates in the stifling heat to greet them. Babylon was presented to Alexander and the people of the city chanted hymns and cast flowers in the path of the young king. The Babylonian cavalry rode forth—not to battle, but to show its finery to Alexander.

The Greek army remained in Babylon a month to rest and to allow wounds received at Gaugamela to mend. The month gave Alexander—who was named "King of the Lands" by the Babylonian priests—ample time to plan his next move. No doubt he gave some thought to the eastern provinces where Darius was now trying to raise another army to meet the invasion. True he had penetrated to the very center of the Persian Empire but there was reason to be aware for a large part of the empire, potentially a dangerous part, had yet to be conquered. In any event Alexander decided that Darius could wait until later. Near the end of November of 331 he gave the order to move out to Susa and, beyond that, toward the mountains of Persia.

Alexander dispatched Philoxenus on ahead to Susa to

arrange for the orderly surrender of that city. As Alexander approached with his army, word was received that all was in order and the Macedonians entered Susa, the spring residence of the Persian kings, without difficulty. The first section of the imperial treasury was uncovered at Susa, netting Alexander some 5,000 talents in silver. The Macedonians also found a number of treasures that had been captured by the Persians in their invasion of Greece. Among them were the sculptured figures of Harmodius and Aristogiton, who, in Athenian legend, were the assassins of the tyrant Hipparchus at the end of the sixth century B.C.

In addition, the Macedonians came across a large throne used by Darius upon which Alexander promptly sat, only to discover that his feet were a good yard off the floor, whereupon he ordered a nearby table placed as a footstool. The Macedonians had not yet learned that Persian thrones were deliberately raised so that the king could tower over the heads of his attending subjects.

From Susa Alexander ascended onto the Iranian plateau where the mountain tribes on the road (the Oxii, Pers, and Huzha), accustomed to exacting blackmail from the king's train, soon learned that a much stronger hand had come to wield the empire. Instead of paying the wild tribesmen for the unhampered passage of his army, Alexander had them hunted down and fined them with a stiff assessment of horses and sheep for their impertinence.

At the Persian Gates, the pass in the mountains that separated Persia proper from the West, Alexander met and defeated a large troop of Persians led by Ariobarzanes and a short time afterwards arrived at Persepolis, the ceremonial capital of the Persian Empire.

According to Plutarch, the treasure that Alexander found at Persepolis was so vast that it took 20,000 mules and 5,000 camels to remove it. The estimated value of the treasure has been determined to equal nearly a quarter billion dollars and when it reached the Greek world it was responsible for the many changes that set the period after Alexander apart from what had gone before, so that his conquest separated the Hellenic from the Hellenistic period in Greek history. The Persepolis treasure financed an explosion of political as well as economic activity, producing operations on a far grander scale than ever before.

Alexander proclaimed himself the monarch of Persia and, taking his seat for the first time under the golden canopy on the royal throne at Persepolis, the young king was aware that not only had the hereditary foe of Greece been utterly defeated, but he was the ruler of the largest empire the world had ever seen. So gladdened was Alexander's old friend, Demaratus of Corinth, when he saw the son of Philip upon the Persian throne that he burst into tears and declared that those Greeks were deprived of great pleasure who had died before seeing Alexander seated on the throne of Darius.

After making a quick journey to Pasargadae where he seized the treasures of Cyrus, Alexander returned to Persepolis and set fire to the royal palace, an act which has been variously estimated by historians. Ostensibly, putting the torches to the beautiful royal palace was Alexander's solemn revenge for the burning of Greek temples by Xerxes, the devastation of Athens, and the slaughter of the Greeks. The burning of the palace has been justified as a symbolic act calculated to impress the imagination of the East, and condemned as a senseless and vainglorious work of destruction. Regardless of his intent in destroying the royal palace (and some sources state that it was not deliberately set afire at all, but was accidentally burned) Alexander made one thing very clear: The rule of the Persians had come to an end.

(Editor's note: Writing in his book, *Persepolis, The*

Archaeology of Jarsa, Seat of the Persian Kings, Donald N. Wilber, the renowned scholar on the ancient and modern Middle East, states: "Although the holocaust of Parsa brought the Achaemenid empire to a sudden and decisive end, there was yet some value in its destruction for very distant, future generations. The masonry elements of its structure and its bas-reliefs were actually protected by the burned debris and the wind-blown dust of the following centuries. They were certainly better protected than they would have been if there had been any unburned buildings remaining above ground, offering inviting opportunities for later builders to carry away the stones.")

With the coming of spring of 330, Alexander not only had the Persian Empire at his feet but he was prepared to settle the matter of King Darius once and for all. He marched north to Ecbatana (modern Hamadan) only to learn that Darius had fled upon his approach. At Ecbatana new masses of treasure were seized. Taking the necessary measures to dispose of the treasure and to establish the occupation of the Median capital, Alexander continued his pursuit, leaving behind his trusted general, Parmenion, to further secure Ecbatana for the empire.

It was an exciting chase, king after king, as Alexander pressed hard at the heels of Darius, each of them covering ground by incredible exertions, shedding their slower traveling followers as they went. It was midsummer when Alexander reached Rhagae (near modern Teheran), just one day's march from the Caspian Gates, only to learn that Darius had already crossed through the gates, losing many deserters as he fled. Alexander rested his army for five days and again took up the chase. It was while he was passing through the Gates that he was told that Darius had been arrested by Bessus, his cousin and a prince of Bactria, and some of his followers.

Leaving behind the major part of his army, Alexander marched through the night and until the next noon, rested a few hours and again marched all night. Along the way he learned that not only had Darius been arrested but Bessus had proclaimed himself and had been hailed king by his Bactrian cavalry and the other Persians in his company. Furthermore Bessus intended to hold Darius hostage and bargain with his person if Alexander continued to pursue the Persian force.

Again Alexander marched all night and until noon the next day as he was now only one day behind the Persians. He ordered his saddlesore cavalry to dismount and stay behind and the infantrymen to take their horses and continue the chase. Taking a shortcut that he had learned about from one of his spies, he came in sight of the broken train at dawn near modern Shahrud. Darius had been bound and tossed in a cart, and was being dragged along by Bessus, but upon the approach of Alexander the Persians fled—though not before Bessus murdered Darius.

Alexander came upon the body of Darius and had it delivered to the queen mother, thus following the example of his idol, Achilles, who, according to Homer, had delivered the body of Hector to his father, Priam.

The pursuit of Darius had brought Alexander into the region of mountains to the south of the Caspian. He had already traversed the western and central provinces of the empire. There now remained only the far eastern provinces, which had been joined but loosely to Persia. He quickly subdued the hill tribes, then marched on, showing the tribes of Hycania, on the southern shores of the Caspian Sea, the power of arms. He brought Parthia under his rule, then turned south and conquered Aria and Drangiana; but in these further provinces of Iran the young king, for the first time, encountered a serious national opposition, for in the East the Persian rule had been merely the supremacy of an alien power over native populations indifferent or hostile. With the power of the Persians broken, home rulers rose up to challenge Alexander.

Alexander learned that Bessus had taken up the diadem as Darius' successor in Bactria (northern Afghanistan), but as soon as he marched his army out against him, Aria rose up behind Alexander and he had to return in all haste to put down the revolt. Finally subduing the eastern provinces, he again turned north to establish his power over Bactria and Sogdiana (Russian Turkestan) but it was on this march that there occurred one of the great tragedies of Alexander's life. This was the conspiracy of Philotas, the son of Parmenion, and the commander of the Macedonian cavalry.

The family of Philotas and Parmenion was ancient and proud and had fought nobly for Philip and Alexander. Parmenion had been permanently assigned to duties at Ecbatana and placed in charge of Alexander's communications, but his duties had been taken over by Craterus. Many of Alexander's followers, notably Philotas and his friends, considered that Alexander had pushed Parmenion aside.

In addition, the old general had grown increasingly out of step with the king's strategy as well as his political ideas. He saw no reason to cross every mountain range or river and had long wished for a contained empire. Then there was the fact of Alexander's increasing personal separation from the members of his command which had been a source of irritation to his generals for some time, and the family of Parmenion seemed to be in the foremost of those who resented Alexander's parade of Persian dress and manners, which Alexander had acquired after Persepolis.

In any event, apparently Philotas thought it was time for the Macedonian nobles to take matters into their own hands, to stop the endless marches and settle down to the enjoyment of their gains. According to Ar-

Alexander charging the bodyguard of Darius at the Battle of Issus

rian, the king accused Philotas of "concealment" and had him brought before the army as the Macedonian law required. He confessed to a plot against Alexander and was killed by the soldiers with their javelins.

Then Alexander had Parmenion put to death at Ecbatana. The death of Parmenion was, to later eyes, an act of cold-blooded murder. Yet Macedonian law decreed that relatives of a conspirator against the king must also die. Probably Alexander decided to let the famous general pay the penalty of the law in order to break the Macedonian opposition against his further conquests.

As a result of Philotas' conspiracy, Alexander decided to let no one again rise to Parmenion's position of power. Philotas' command was split between Hephaestion, the favorite among Alexander's Companions, and Cleitus the Black, the two the king most trusted. By the winter of 330-29, Alexander had reached the Kabul Valley at the foot of the Paropamisadae (Hindu Kush).

In the spring of 329 Alexander crossed the Hindu Kush into Bactria and followed the retreat of Bessus across the Oxus and into Sogdiana, where Alexander received word that Bessus had been arrested by his followers. Bessus was delivered to Alexander and sent back to Bactria-Zariaspa to await judgment. Then Alexander marched to Maracanda (modern Samarkand) from which he conducted a number of forays in all directions and remained in the area to found Alexandria Eschate, the "farthest" of his Greek cities.

It was at Maracanda that the second great tragedy occurred in Alexander's life. After sacrificing to the divine twins, Castor and Pollux, for victories over the people of the steppes, there was a drinking party at which flatterers got the king's ear with observation that Castor and Pollux, even Heracles, were nothing beside Alexander.

Such talk distressed Cleitus the Black, Alexander's

boyhood friend. He became upset by the Persian barbarism that Alexander had affected and the Greek flatterers who belittled gods and heroes to overrate Alexander. He thought the king could have done nothing without his Macedonian followers and said so. The conversation grew heated with comparisons of Alexander to various gods and even to his father, Philip, which caused Cleitus to minimize Alexander in rather strong terms whereupon Alexander grabbed a pike and ran it through Cleitus' body.

Alexander, once sober, lay lamenting on his couch for three days, calling himself a slayer of friends and refusing to eat or drink until all about him were frightened of losing his leadership. Finally the king aroused himself and went on but now all saw that direct exchange of free opinion with Alexander was no longer possible.

The spring of 327 saw the last of Alexander's campaigns beyond the Hindu Kush. The one remaining outpost of resistance north of the Oxus was the Sogdian Rock, held by the forces of Oxyartes who had accompanied Bessus and still held the scattered remnants of his army. But once confronted with Alexander's army, Oxyartes surrendered. Alexander had now spent two years trying to placate the rebels of Bactria-Sogdiana. Obviously a solution other than the constant skirmishes had to be found and Alexander found it at Sogdian Rock.

Among the people in the settlement was Oxyartes' beautiful daughter, Roxane. His solution to the rebel problem was to marry her. Legend would later turn it into a love affair but it was purely a political marriage, and the beginning of Alexander's effort to take Asia into full partnership with him. The latter and a desire to legitimize his rule led him, three years later, to marry Barsine, the daughter of Darius. At that time 10,000 of his soldiers took Asian wives.

Not only did Oxyartes sanction the marriage of his daughter to the king, but two of his sons joined the Macedonian forces along with contingents of Bactrian, Sogdian, and Scythian cavalry, which the king was quick to accept, having learned of their effectiveness in his two-year-long running battle with them. By the summer of 327 Alexander had once more crossed the Hindu Kush on his way to India.

Alexander crossed the Indus, and proceeded through the Punjab to the river Hydaspes (now known as the Jhelum), to a country dominated by three principalities —that of Ambhi, between the Indus and Hydaspes, centered in the great city of Taxila, that of the Paurara rajah, between the Hydaspes and Acesines, and that of Abhisara between the same two rivers higher up, on the confines of Kashmir. Alexander reached the Hydaspes just as the rains broke, when the river was already swollen. Porus, the most able king of the East, was prepared to contest the passage of the river with all his strength and held the opposite bank with a large army, including 200 elephants.

Alexander succeeded in taking a part of his army across the swollen river during a night of torrential rain, and then he fought the fourth and last of his major battles in Asia, the one which put to proof more shrewdly than any of the others the quality of the Macedonian army as an instrument of war, and yet again emerged victorious. Porus fell sorely wounded into Alexander's hands and the young king was so struck by the royal bearing of the aged Indian rajah that he made him viceroy of the conquered portion of India east of the Indus. The country west of the Indus he placed under the rule of Macedonian governors.

Leaving Craterus at the Hydaspes to prepare vessels and supplies for moving downriver, Alexander, with the rest of his army, traveled eastward to cross the Acesines (modern Chenab), where he left Hephaestion

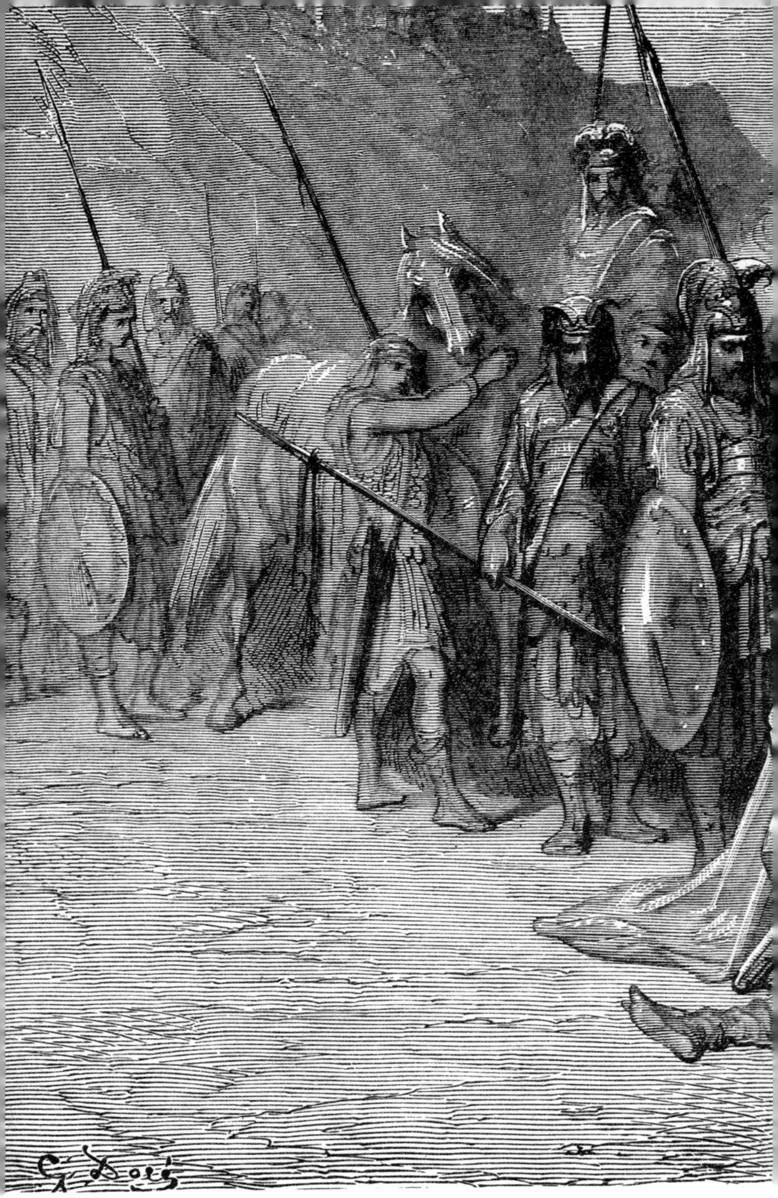
G. Doré

Alexander discovering the body of the Persian king Darius

to fortify a city. As Alexander's army proceeded, they received submission from some of the peoples they encountered, and had to fight others, but Alexander pushed on, convinced that the ocean was just beyond the last of the tributaries of the Indus and that once he reached it he would have taken the eastern end of the world.

However, at the Beas River, the Macedonian army—gazing across the interminable plains extending to the horizon, their spirits low—refused to go on. During the past eight and a half years they had marched 11,000 miles and were fatigued, mentally and physically, and could not see the purpose of further marching and fighting in unknown lands. For three days the will of Alexander and that of his army was locked in antagonism, then the king gave in and the long eastward movement came, finally, to an end; the return began.

To mark the farthest point of his advance, Alexander erected 12 tremendous altars to the Olympian gods and offered sacrifice upon them, then celebrated gymnastic and cavalry contests. He also prepared armor that was larger than that used by his army, stalls for horses that were higher, and bits that were heavier than those in common use—and left them scattered near the river so that later generations would be impressed with the manner of men who had come that way.

Alexander and his army retraced their steps to the Hydaspes where he had left Craterus to prepare for the river descent, which began in November of 326. Alexander had the pick of his troops with him on board the equally spaced ships while Craterus followed along on the right bank with one infantry battalion and the cavalry; Hephaestion was on the left with the remainder of the troops and the elephants. Undoubtedly Alexander purposely placed his two generals on opposite sides of the river for the rivalry between them had reached a point where they had recently nearly come to blows. Hephaestion, the elder in years and the king's favorite, resented the younger and more able Craterus. Following the troops was the baggage and bringing up the rear was a vast host of Indian princes and their retinues, women, children, and traders.

Once the confluence of the Hydaspes and Acesines was passed the Macedonians again found themselves in a region of hostile tribes with towns that had to be stormed. It was at one of these, a town of the Malli, that Alexander's army all but gave up the fight. Seeing the hesitation, Alexander grabbed a ladder and raced up it to the top of the citadel wall, behind which the rebels were holding out. Three of his men followed to protect him, which spurred others to follow them but they broke the ladder, leaving Alexander and his three bodyguards stranded on the wall.

Alexander was struck on the head and, as he sagged, was severely wounded by a long arrow that pierced a lung. As one of his men covered him with the shield of Achilles, another threatened any of the Mallians who might care to press their advantage until the army, now at a frenzy, burst through the walls and killed all the defenders.

Alexander was carried out more dead than alive. The king recovered after several days, then continued his journey, which was to become one of the greatest marches in military history. Down the Indus and through the sands of Gedrosia and Carmania, his army marched back to Persepolis, which they reached after much hardship early in 324 B.C., while his fleet explored anew the ancient water routes from the Indus to the Euphrates. Alexander repaired to Babylon, now the capital of his newly conquered world.

On his return to Babylon Alexander did not rest. He hoped to push his conquests into Arabia, and to give a firmer organization to his empire, the machine of which had not functioned altogether smoothly while the king had been absent, and on Alexander's return many incapables and rogues in high office had to be replaced by better men.

New orders and appointments served to quickly bring the empire into hand again and, finally, at Susa in the spring of 324, Alexander rested and married Barsine. The marriage to the daughter of Darius which was occasioned by the simultaneous marriage of 10,000 of his men to Persian women did little to allay the discontent of the Macedonian army, and when Alexander moved to the cooler region of Media in the summer of 324, a mutiny broke out among the Macedonians accompanying him.

At Ecbatana the death of Hephaestion plunged the king into a long passion of mourning that lasted for weeks. But by the winter of 324-323 B.C. Alexander was again active and embarked upon a campaign against the Uxians and Cossaeans, still restive in the area southeast of Ecbatana.

In the spring of 323 B.C. Alexander moved down to Babylon, receiving on the way embassies from lands as far as the confines of the known world, for the eyes of all nations now turned with fear or wonder to the figure which had appeared with such superhuman effect upon the world's stage. Once in Babylon, he entered upon a round of activity. The exploration of the waterways roundabout the empire was his immediate concern, the discovery of the presumed connection of the Caspian Sea with the Northern Ocean, the opening of a maritime route from Babylon to Egypt around Arabia.

The latter enterprise Alexander designed to conduct in person and prepared a vast fleet under his direct supervision. When all was ready and a date was set for departure of the fleet, Alexander made sacrifices and caroused deep into the night for two days running. He fell ill with a fever only three days before the time set for departure but treated his illness as a momentary impediment to the expedition. However, a week later he had lost his voice and the Macedonian army was suffered to pass man by man through his chamber and bid him farewell. On June 13 of 323 B.C., Alexander died at Babylon, not yet 33 years of age, after a reign of only 12 years and eight months.

The world was never again to be the same. Gone was the Greek city-state and the homogeneous civilization concentrated around the Aegean Sea.

Alexander was more than just a conqueror. He had a vision of making all the people of the world one, one race under one government (hence the frequent appointment of natives to positions of power in his conquered provinces and the marriages—his own and that of 10,000 of his troops—to Asian women). Plutarch, writing 400 years later said: "If the power [daemon] which sent the soul of Alexander into this world had not been in such a hurry to recall it, one law would now be looking down upon all men and they would turn their gaze upon one system of justice as though upon a light which all could see, and thus would they be governed. But, as things turned out, part of the world remained unlit by the sun—the part which never saw Alexander."

True, the empire broke up after Alexander's death and was carved into four major and numerous minor empires, but the new kingdoms were ruled by Macedonians and Greeks for three centuries until the coming of Rome. By breaking down the barriers which had separated the Greeks and the "barbarians" Alexander paved the way for the spread of a higher culture, a culture that would civilize Rome and facilitate her creation of a world state and finally the conquest of that state by Christianity.

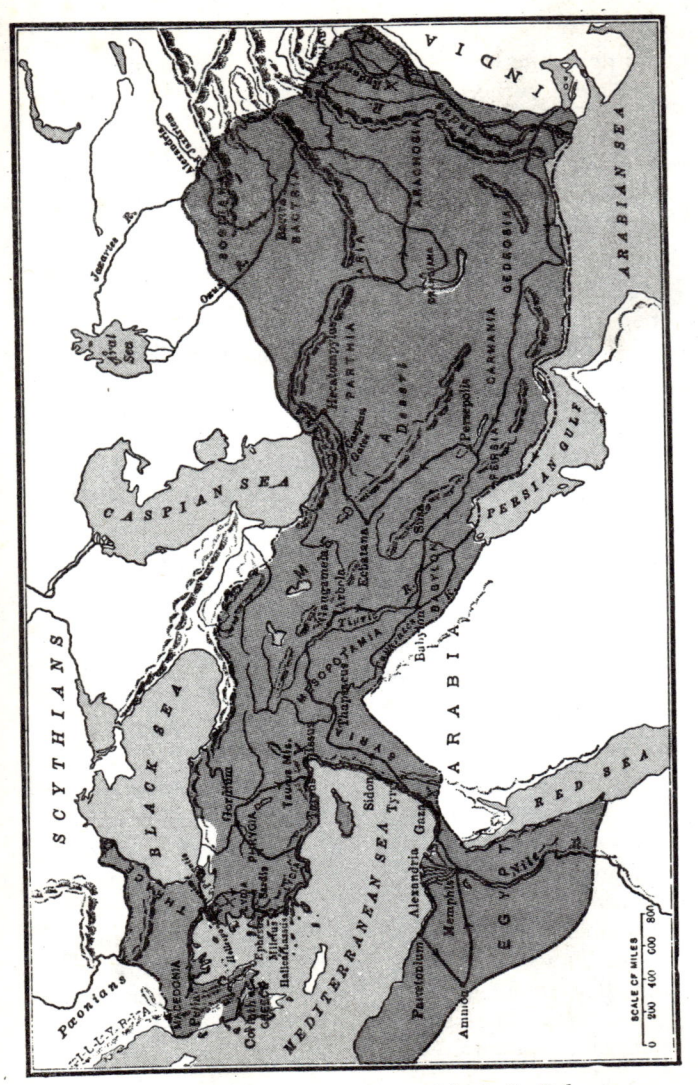

The Empire of Alexander the Great (shaded). Following Alexander's death and years of war and intrigue, the Empire was divided among four of Alexander's generals.

A LEGENDARY VIEW OF ALEXANDER

By Ronald Leal

*T*he great structure of legend that grew up around the life and exploits of Alexander the Great began shortly after his death and, by the Middle Ages, had come to make up a body of literature of overwhelming proportions. Writers, poets, and artists of Medieval Europe so embroidered the ancient accounts of Alexander's conquest that they all but obscured the true tale of his exploits. Their efforts, which came to be known as the Romance of Alexander, eventually constituted a literature separate from, yet based upon, the known facts of the conqueror's life, that was eventually circulated in some 80 versions, at least two dozen languages, and spread from Iceland to the Far East.

But the medieval writers and those of the Orient—who always looked upon Alexander as more than a man

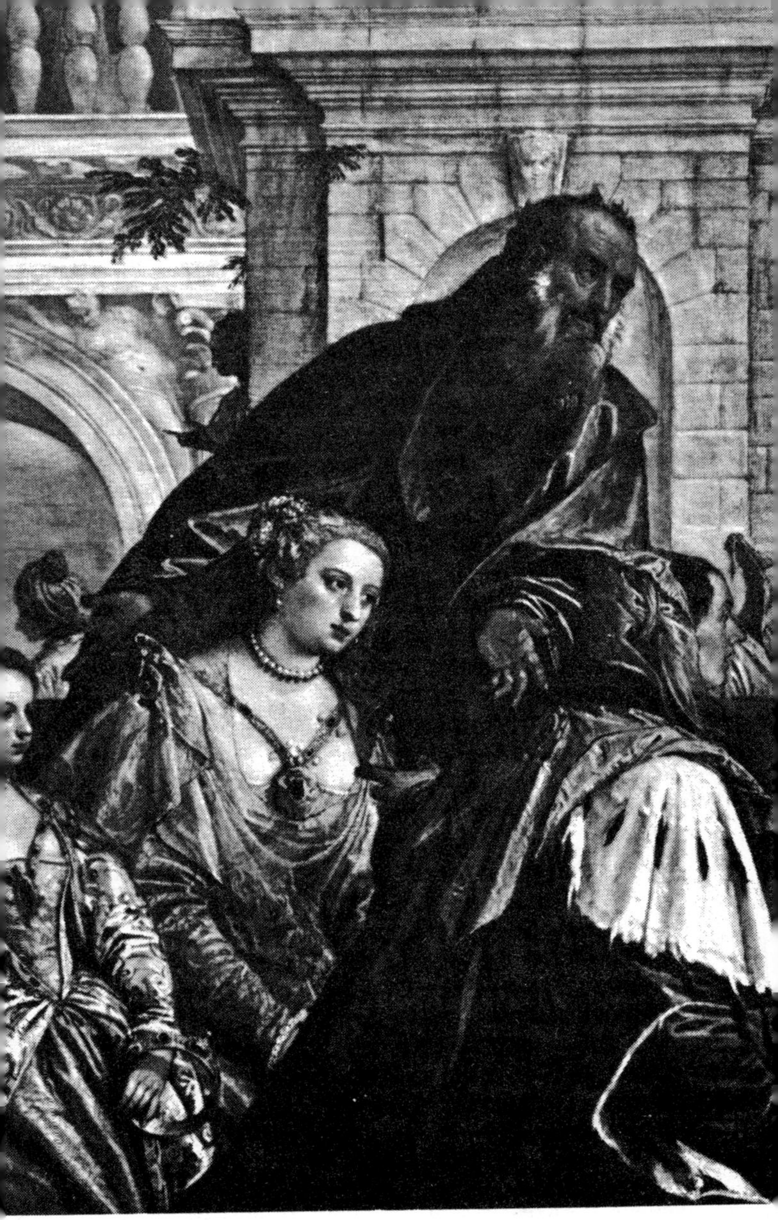

Alexander before the family of Darius

if not exactly a god—certainly had precedents for their Romance. Plutarch (A.D. 46?–A.D. 120?), the Greek essayist and biographer, drawing upon contemporary accounts, gave voice to many of the myths that would later be accepted as fact. Who but a god could be "descended from Hercules by Carnus [on his father's side] from Aeacus by Neoptolemus on his mother's side" as reported by Plutarch?

According to the Greek biographer, the night before the consummation of her marriage Alexander's mother, Olympias, "dreamed that a thunderbolt fell upon her body, which kindled a great fire, whose divided flames dispersed themselves all about and then were extinguished." And Philip, soon after he was married, "dreamt that he sealed his wife's body with a seal, whose impression, as he fancied, was the figure of a lion . . . Aristander of Telmessus, considering how unusual it was to seal up anything that was empty, assured him the meaning of his dream was that the queen was with child of a boy, who would one day prove as stout and courageous as a lion." It would later be said that on the night of Alexander's birth "the air changed color . . . thunder and lightning shook the earth . . . animals shivered with fear and everything trembled . . . because he would conquer and rule all things . . . and wise men gathered together to discuss the strange portents." It was said, too, that when Olympias delivered her baby, thirty other princes were born in Greece and surrounding countries who were to become Alexander's future Companions and eventually his officers. Later it would be said that Alexander's father was not Philip of Macedonia, but was the god Zeus. This last bit of fancy was indulged in by Olympias herself and told by her to Philip.

Aristoxenus gave further evidence of Alexander's godlike qualities in his Memoirs: "A most agreeable odour exhaled from his skin, his breath and body all over were so fragrant as to perfume the clothes which he wore next to him; the cause of which might probably be the hot and adust temperament of his body."

We are told that when Alexander was ready to begin his Persian campaign many portents from Heaven were reported. When he went to Delphi to consult Apollo concerning the success of the war, the priestess there said to him, "My son, thou art invincible." Whereupon Alexander declared he had received such an answer as he wished for and it was needless to consult the god any further. Among other prodigies that attended the departure of his army, the image of Orpheus at Libethra, made of cypress wood, was "seen to sweat in great abundance, to the discouragement of many." But Aristander told him that, far from presaging any ill to him, it signified he should perform acts so important and glorious as would make the poets and musicians of future ages labour and sweat to describe and celebrate them."

There is also the legend, as reported by Plutarch, that after the battle of the Granicus, when Alexander moved his army south to secure the Persian maritime provinces, he "passed his army along the seacoasts of Pamphylia . . . and the waves which usually come rolling in violently from the main, and hardly ever leave so much as a narrow beach under the steep, broken cliffs at any time uncovered, should on a sudden retire to afford him passage." Menander, in one of his comedies, alludes to this marvel when he says:

"Was Alexander ever favoured more?
Each man I wish for meets me at my door.
And should I ask for passage through the sea,
The sea I doubt not would retire for me."

Plutarch prudently points out that Alexander's epistles "mention nothing unusual in this at all, but he says he went from Phaselis, and passed through what they call the Ladders." We may safely assume that al-

A LEGENDARY VIEW OF ALEXANDER

ready in Plutarch's time Alexander's exploits were being looked upon as if blessed with divine favor.

The legend that most stirred the imagination of medieval artists was the meeting of Alexander and the family of Darius who were captured after the battle of Issus. Dozens of beautiful paintings were made of the legendary meeting, all depicting, in elegant medieval splendor, either the wife or the mother of Darius before Alexander. Yet, there is not one shred of evidence that such a meeting ever took place (although years later Alexander did marry Darius' daughter, Barsine). In a letter to his general, Parmenio, Alexander said he "had not so much as seen or desired to see the wife of Darius [reputedly the most beautiful woman in Asia], no, nor suffered anybody to speak of her beauty before him."

Alexander himself gave fuel to many of the later legends, often by telling of his dreams, such as the one he reported during the siege of Tyre when he said that he "dreamt that he saw Hercules upon the walls [of Tyre], reaching out his hands and calling to me."

There is also the report of his journey to visit Zeus Ammon, the famous Oracle of Siwa in the Libyan Desert. During this journey, according to Plutarch, "the relief and assistance the gods afford him in his distresses were more remarkable, and obtained greater belief than the oracles he received afterwards, for first, plentiful rains that fell [in the desert] preserved them from any fear of perishing by drought, and, allaying the extreme dryness of the sand, which now became moist and firm to travel on, cleared and purified the air." He continues by saying that when Alexander's guides lost their way, they were set right again by some ravens "which flew before them when on the march, and waited for them when they lingered and fell behind; and the greatest miracle, as Callisthenes tells us, was that if any of the company went astray in the night, they [the ravens] never ceased croaking and making a noise till by that means they had brought them into the right way again."

The Romance of Alexander so appealed to the fifteenth-century Dukes of Burgundy that they commissioned the finest French artists to illustrate the story in hundreds of miniatures, one of which showed Alexander descending to the bottom of the sea in a wire cage so that he might "know all that is beneath the waters as well as that which is on land." And of such flights of imagination came the legends of Alexander.

Augustus

THE AGE OF AUGUSTUS

By Marvin Berry

*F*ew men in Western Man's past have so determined subsequent events as did the Roman Emperor Augustus. As an individual who came to power when the Roman state was in total collapse, he can rank with others who, in times of peril, responded to a challenge, gave new direction and subsequently altered the flow of history. His solutions to the many problems which had rent asunder the Empire for over a century left an indelible mark on the Empire for the rest of its history.

The cancers plaguing the Roman world when Octavian Caesar gained absolute power in 31 B.C. were so rampant, ingrained and seemingly so insoluble that one could not help but think that man had reached the mythological Age of Iron, an age noted for unbridled violence and for the total absence of justice and morality. Octavian pulled the Roman people and Empire from this quagmire, rescued them from unmitigated chaos, and gave to his people a peace that would last for centuries.

For over a century before his ascendency the Mediterranean world, and especially Italy, had endured convulsive turmoil. During this period, for the first time, Romans had fought Romans, military and political traditions were cast aside and leaders appeared who were much more concerned with personal aggrandizement than with the state. The cause for this is easy to find: the Roman people had undergone remarkable changes, changes created, in a sense, by the awesome military successes Rome had achieved as she developed from a small city state to become the mistress of Italy and the Mediterranean Sea.

Tradition held that the Romans were descendants of a Trojan Prince, Aeneas, who, escaping the Trojan War in the twelfth century B.C., had fled to Italy and had settled in the rolling hills south of the Tiber River. Some three centuries later twin brothers had been born to a Vestal Virgin, a descendant of Aeneas. One of these brothers, Romulus, had moved to the Tiber River and built Rome as a city for himself and his men. The traditional date for this was 753 B.C.

The city grew quickly. It was located on a site that served as an excellent link between the Etruscan civilization to its north and the ever increasing Greek colonies to its south. After the reign of four native kings, Rome succumbed to Etruscan domination. Three alien Etruscan rulers so aroused the hatred of the Romans that the last one was overthrown. With this event, around 510 B.C., the Romans marked the beginning of their Republic.

Determined to preclude ever again the rise of a monarchy the executive power was henceforth shared by two chief magistrates, known first as praetors and subsequently as consuls. To limit their powers these two magistrates had to agree on all actions taken and, as all other magistrates, could serve only one year in office.

The other primary magistracies were the praetorship, aedileship and quaestorship. The duties involved with each developed over the centuries. By the time of the second century B.C., the functions, generally, were: the praetors were the judges, the aediles were concerned with maintenance of the city and the quaestors were involved with financial matters. In emergencies a dictator could be named to solve the crisis of the moment.

To secure herself from any further attempt by the Extruscans to dominate her, Rome entered into an alliance with neighboring states. This alliance, known as the Latin League, proved effective. But it required, however, on the part of all, a military preparedness that put an important role on the citizens who made up the army. This need did not escape the notice of the people: they began to demand political rights which the Senatorial landowners were loathe to grant. With no choice under the circumstances, the Senate relented and gave to the people the right to have an official who could attend to their needs. Around 475 B.C., this office, the tribunate, was established with the power to veto the action of any magistrate which seemed dangerous to the interests of the people. For the moment the people were satisfied.

As another generation came along, though, other problems came forth. Especially did the plebeians chafe under the arbitrary judicial decisions handed down by the noble judges. The masses demanded a written law to permit them to know that by which they were judged. A committee was created to achieve this end. In 450 B.C., the renowned Law of the Twelve Tables was promulgated. Only five years later another grant was given to the commons: they could now marry into the Senatorial order, a right beneficial to both sides. The Senators, by tradition, could pursue no occupation other than farming. This taboo left to the people the virtually exclusive right to pursue trading and commerce. This had been rewarding to all thus involved, because of Rome's location as a trade center between northern and southern Italy. With intermarriage now allowed, the wealth of the merchant class could find its way into Senatorial families.

About fifty years thereafter a devastating blow arrested the peaceful development of Rome and her allies. From the north a destructive invasion by peoples known as Gauls caused consternation. The Etruscans melted before them. In 390 B.C., Rome was sacked by them. The consequences were alarming. The Latin League withdrew from Rome's leadership, feeling that Rome had been impotent at a time when she was most needed. This secession Rome could not allow; she could not be placed in such an untenable, unprotected position. Fortunately the Gauls withdrew and no other threat diverted Rome's energies from putting down the rebellion among her allies. This was finally done in 338 B.C.

One solution, however, seemed to evoke another crisis. The fierce Samnites, living along the Appenine Mountains, resented the growing military power of a people so close to them. From 325 B.C. to 290 B.C., Rome had to fight these tribes to secure her western borders. In the end the Samnites reluctantly submitted to Rome.

It was during this period that one of the most impressive figures in Rome's Republican history lived. The famous Appius Claudius, a hero of the Samnite Wars, had begun a road to facilitate the flow of troops and materiel. So well was this road, the Appian Way, constructed that now, twenty-three hundred years later, it is still in use.

In fear of Rome's encroaching military might the Greek city-states in southern Italy began to look for aid. They found a willing ally from the Greek world who thought that, by keeping Rome from marching farther south, he, Pyrrhus, king of Epirus, could gain dominant influence in this wealthy agricultural part of Italy. This Pyrrhus had been one of the many generals who had vied with others for supremacy over Greece after the sudden untimely death of Alexander the Great in 323 B.C. He had managed to secure Epirus unto himself, the country from whence Alexander's mother had originally come.

Eager to increase his prestige Pyrrhus entered Italy in 281 B.C., to aid the Greek cities. Against him, though, Rome held her own militarily—a remarkable achievement as she was fighting the heir to the military technocracy of Alexander. Finally she defeated Pyrrhus who withdrew from Italy in 270 B.C.

Rome now controlled all of southern Italy and, at the same time, had extended her influence over the northern areas of the peninsula, filling the void created by the gradual decline of Etruscan power.

In the 120 years between 390 and 270 B.C., the remarkable had occurred. From the time of the destructive Gallic sack of the city Rome had been forced to fight for her survival. She had put the Latin League under her control and given the various states specified treaty rights, she had conquered the Samnites, she had defeated the Greek genius, Pyrrhus, and had extended her hold over all of Italy south of the Po Valley. No land power could now surpass the army of the Roman people or question her control over Italy. Interestingly, each march forward had been for defensive reasons.

During this same period additional rights had been granted to the plebeians. They had won the right that one of their number could hold one of the two consulships each year, the conservative priesthoods were opened to their ranks and finally, just before the Pyrrhic invasion, it was allowed that any bill that the commons passed in their assembly became law, with or without the approval of the Senate. In view of this the masses and the treaty states had every reason to fight an invader undauntingly. Such a political development was to be even more important in the events of the next seventy years. Within six years Rome became involved in quarrels between the mightiest maritime power of the day, Carthage, and the brilliant city-state of Syracuse. War began between Carthage and Rome in 264 B.C., a war called, after Carthage's Phoenician origin, the First Punic War. After a see-saw struggle, Rome was victorious; Syracuse came out for Rome and aided in the building of Rome's first navy; nature aided Rome when storms debilitated Carthage's fleet. When the war ended in 241 B.C., Rome found herself now to be the naval power of the western Mediterranean. She had control of Sicily, Corsica and Sardinia. Carthage lay at her feet, with harsh terms meted out by the Romans. The ultimate blow to Carthage was that she was forbidden to rebuild her fleet.

Smarting under this defeat the next generation of Carthaginians were determined to seek vengeance. Under the mighty Hannibal Carthage invaded Italy in 218, coming by land (since she still had no navy) across the Pyrenees and Alpine passes. Hannibal confidently felt that the Italian allies of Rome would turn to him for their "freedom" from Roman influence. In this he was sadly disappointed; he did not know how strongly the Roman allies were bound to Rome. He got little aid from them. Nevertheless, the confusion in the Roman leadership nearly brought disaster. Hannibal brilliantly destroyed two Roman armies sent against him, one in 217 near the beautiful Lake Trasimene and another in 216 in southeastern Italy, at Cannae. Fearing now to commit themselves to open combat the Romans began a guerrilla type of warfare. Hannibal could not achieve his main goal of attacking Rome itself. His supplies and reinforcements were becoming critical and the leadership in Carthage was becoming impatient. A reserve army under Hannibal's brother was intercepted and defeated. Hannibal was recalled; he fled to the Kingdom of Syria, as Rome came forth in 202 B.C. once again.

The ever growing military and naval power of Rome seemed to know no limit. While she was engaged in the agonizing struggle with Hannibal, she was forced into the Greek world. The king of Macedonia, Philip V, had entered into an alliance with Carthage. Rome was able to keep any aid from coming to Hannibal, and, a few years after the Second Punic War was over, she prevented Philip from having any dominant control over Greece proper. Philip's son, Perseus, ambitious and determined to gain mastery over Greece, provoked a war with Rome in 171 B.C. Three years later Rome conquered Macedonia, destroyed the monarchy and ended Macedonia's influence in ancient history.

Several significant, and ominous, factors now emerged. In Rome's political development there had been, for the masses, a gradual, liberalizing tone. Due, though, to the Hannibalic threat the masses had willingly turned the leadership of the state over to the knowledgeable nobility. The plebeians began to lose influence in the political realm, for debate and crises strengthened the Senatorial executives. Their position was further exacerbated by the guerrilla warfare throughout Italy; farms, large and small, were destroyed. The farmers were needed for the army and this, too, permitted many farms to go unattended. When the war ended the farmers possessed no capital with which to pick up anew. With nothing to do, many drifted to Rome where it was evident that the Senatorial leadership was determined to maintain its total domination over the state.

The wealth of the conquests was pouring into coffers over which the Senate had complete control. More and more the nobility was the only group who could afford election to magistracies and who had the capital with which to invest. Invariably the available farmland in Italy and in conquered territories was purchased by wealthy Senators and made into huge estates. The government of the territories, or provinces, became a Senatorial monopoly. An ex-magistrate could go forth as a governor with absolute power over his province. Even after depositing a predetermined amount of taxes in the state treasury, a governor could return home a millionaire.

The increasing polarization of the classes, the insensitivity of the nobility and the growing restlessness of the Roman allied states in Italy over the inferior treatment accorded them created an atmosphere of distrust. The tranquillity of the state was threatened. Only a spark was needed to create a holocaust.

In 149 B.C., the Senate provoked, for no good reason, a third war with Carthage. The cause could only be that many of the Senators feared Carthage's remarkable agricultural productivity, hardly a threat to Rome politically or militarily. The city was nevertheless sacked in 146 B.C., leveled to the ground and accursed, with tons of salt strewn over her farmlands. The Senate had shown again its arrogance in this uncalled-for destruction. For the first time in Rome's history a war was waged that had not been of a general defensive nature.

During these same three years Rome conquered the bickering Greek city-states and made Greece a province. Macedonia had proved to be troublesome even after Perseus's defeat; she now was made a province of the Empire. In this manner more provinces, and hence, more wealth were added to Senatorial control.

A young man, Tiberius Gracchus, of illustrious background, for he was the grandson of Scipio Africanus, the victor of the Hannibalic war, happened to return

THE AGE OF AUGUSTUS

through the farmlands of Italy on his way home from the Third Punic War. He noticed the poverty of the farmers and allies of Rome. He was convinced that land reform was essential to the well-being of the state. Why, he thought, must the lower classes continue to fight for Rome and, in the end, have no place to rest their heads? He decided to seek election as tribune and in this capacity to present a reform program.

His plan was aided by the death of Attalus III, the king of the wealthy kingdom of Pergamun, the area near ancient Troy. Attalus had seen the inexorable when Rome entered Greece in 146 B.C. He knew Rome's control over the Aegean Sea would be absolute. As he had no heir he feared strife would erupt in his kingdom upon his death and, to avoid this, he bequeathed his kingdom to the Roman people. This bequest gave Rome incalculable monies as well as control over the Dardanelles. Tiberius, as tribune in the year 133 B.C., proposed that land be purchased from estate holders with the wealth of Pergamum and then be redistributed among the poor. As rational and as legal as this proposal was the Senate viciously opposed it. When Tiberius stood for election for a consecutive term as tribune, thereby breaking the Republic's custom of a one-year tenure in office, armed Senators attacked and killed the idealistic reformer.

Ten years later in 123 B.C. Tiberius' younger brother Gaius entered upon the tribunate. He was eager to avenge his brother's murder, to make the tribunate a vital civil office, to extend the citizenship to worthy allies, to implement his brother's land reform and to aid the poor through a system of state-supported doles. Successful at first, he stood for re-election for 122 B.C. His brother had paved the way; no serious incident occurred in his re-election. Trouble did develop, though, when the proposal for the extension of the citizenship was discussed. The business element did not like the idea of thousands of non-Romans possibly holding the key to elections. Gaius lost the support of commercial interests and was defeated in his bid for election for the third time. Attacks against his program increased. Martial law was declared. His followers were hounded and Gaius himself committed suicide rather than fall into the hands of his enemies.

For the first time now Roman was fighting Roman. For one century after this no generation would fail to be involved in civil war. The Senate would be ever recalcitrant. The masses would incessantly demand their due and follow leaders who promised to aid them. The provincial governments, reflecting the chaos of the capital, would be more and more corrupt. And worse, the legions of Rome would give loyalty only to those who could give them rewards. Such was the tone of the century before Augustus.

One looks at the turmoil of this age and wonders how any state could have survived. The corruption, dissension, greed and plays for power would seem to preclude any justification for its survival. Yet, in spite of this, underneath there remained the basic Roman character: stern, unyielding, fond of the soil of Italy, respecting discipline and law. These virtues, once a chance was given for them to appear, would stand in good stead for Augustus.

Nor is it without reason that this age of chaos produced the most brilliant leaders and writers of vital and inimitable masterpieces of literature: an age of crisis can evoke the best as well as the worst in a people. Brilliant politicians and men of letters—Cicero, Lucretius, Catullus, Sallust, Julius Caesar and Pompey the Great—stand out as familiar figures from this period.

A decade after the death of Gaius Gracchus, one Jugurtha had gained the crown of Numidia, an African kingdom near Carthage, through unscrupulous murders and intrigues. In his rise he had killed many Roman and Italian merchants and had greatly interfered with

THE AGE OF AUGUSTUS

trade in this area. After delays, in 111 B.C., the Senate sent an army to restrain him; Jugurtha defeated it and found it easy to bribe the Roman leaders, even declaring that any Roman could be bribed. The Senate's inability to control Jugurtha quickly cost it the confidence of the business class, which urged that such a threat be repressed.

A man of plebeian rank, who had married the aunt of Julius Caesar, emerged and united the masses and the business interests. This Marius, with their support, was elected Consul in 107 B.C. In spite of Senatorial opposition, he was given the command to pursue the war with Jugurtha. He brought it to a dramatic close with the help of one of his lieutenants, Sulla, who captured the King. Marius returned in triumph to Rome as the victor and as the champion of the masses.

At this time panic had struck the city. Germanic tribes were on the verge of moving into Italy. Marius was chosen to fight them and, defying all precedents and custom, was elected Consul for four years in succession, 104-101 B.C. He defeated the tribes, returned in triumph again and was hailed as savior of Rome.

Such power and success for one of plebeian rank terrified the Senate. Marius had virtually established a one-man rule, with his power based on the support of the masses and on his armies.

Meanwhile, the military crisis had shown to Marius the urgency of reforms in the army. He began to enlist men for a term of sixteen years; he cast aside restrictions on eligibility; he established a vigorous training program and he assured his men that he would see to it that they were rewarded with land and pensions after their term of service. The army now, obviously, would give its ultimate loyalty to its commander rather than to the state. In this development the stage was prepared for other war lords to emerge in the future.

Other events revealed more problems.

A massive slave rebellion occurred in Sicily in 105 B.C. and lasted four years. The dangers of slave labor throughout the large landed estates became evident.

In another instance a total disregard for traditional values was revealed when an honorable noble, Rutilius Rufus, was brought to trial, and convicted, on the charge of extortion as proconsular governor of Asia. His only crime had been that, as governor, he forbade and suppressed illegal tax collections gleaned by businessmen and fiscal agents. So enraged were they at this interference that they were determined to show that no governor could, with impunity, stop them from ravaging any province at will. Rufus went into exile, living the rest of his life as the honored "guest" of the province he was said to have plundered

Another nobleman, Livius Drusus, moved by the aims of the Gracchi and trying, legally, to effect a solution to the growing disparity among the classes, proposed that the Senate allow more of the business class to be represented in the Senate, that a dole be given to the masses, that colonies be founded to alleviate crowded conditions in the city and that Roman citizenship be extended to the Italian allies who had fought so long for Rome. He was murdered by an unknown assassin.

Unhappily this was to be the last chance Rome would have to remedy social ills by peaceful and legal means. The only other way would be through civil strife and war.

Rebuffed by the death of Drusus in their attempts to gain the rights of citizenship, the allies rebelled. A new state, Italia, was created in 90 B.C. For three years Rome attempted to suppress the rebellion. Failing this and alarmed by the rise of a powerful king in Asia Minor, Rome capitulated and granted citizenship to her Italian allies. To achieve this a useless, needless war had occurred and the jealousy with which the Romans viewed their citizenship rights was revealed, along with her haughty attitude toward her allies.

THE AGE OF AUGUSTUS

Roman power in the Aegean had grown constantly for sixty years since Greece and Pergamum had become provinces. Resenting this, Mithridates V of Pontus had determined to obliterate Rome's influence near his kingdom. In 88 B.C. the King invaded Western Asia Minor, gained control of the Aegean and encouraged the Greeks to rebel. Athens did so. When he massacred all Romans in Asia Minor, the Senate had to act. The Consul, Sulla, Marius's former aide, was given the command because of his unquestioned loyalty to, and support of, the Senate. The masses, though, preferred Marius, and their leaders tried to depose Sulla. Sulla heard of this when he had already left Rome for the East. He ordered his army to return to Rome; he entered the city and killed the leaders who had spoken against him. For the first time in Rome's history the inviolable tradition that no army could enter the city gates had been cast aside and for the first time an army had been used to solve a political problem. Sulla departed again for the East. Marius's followers took over the city and murdered Sulla's adherents.

In 83 B.C. Sulla returned victorious, invaded the city for the second time and began a calculated and unrestricted murder of Marius's followers. The Roman Forum flowed with Roman blood. Over five thousand people were murdered, their property and possessions confiscated.

All powerful now, Sulla was given dictatorial powers and, following the precedent of the committee authorized to draw up the Law of the Twelve Tables, he was given the power to revise completely the constitution. In this he was determined that the Senate would be all powerful. He forbade the re-election to an office unless ten years had intervened. He forbade anyone who should be a tribune to be eligible for any other office. He restored veto power over legislation to the Senate. When he had thus emasculated the rights of the masses and had seen to it that no future Gracchi or Marius would emerge and that the Senate was supreme, he resigned in 79 B.C., retired, worked on his memoirs and died a year later.

The Senate took great comfort in its restored authority. At no time, though, does it seem to have been more impossible for this self-centered body to have resolved the vexing problems of the state. Debt, poverty, agrarian problems, maltreated provinces, discontented masses, unemployment and downtrodden slaves were still very evident. The widespread need for solutions permitted a new generation of ambitious, eager men to gain favor and power. Now emerge Pompey the Great, Julius Caesar, Cicero, Antony and Octavian.

The Senate turned to Pompey, Sulla's protege, as its leader. Though a vain and proud man he was still one of great military ability and, unusual for the time, one of some principle.

His first concern was to repress a rebellion in Spain. A follower of Marius, Sertorius, had made Spain his personal kingdom, hoping to govern it independent of the Senate. So wisely did he, in fact, rule that the Spaniards willingly followed him. Determined to punish such a threat to the state the Senate sent several armies against Sertorius. He withstood them for seven years. Only when he was assassinated by a friend did Pompey emerge victorious in 71 B.C.

On his return to Italy Pompey was caught in the final battles of Roman armies, under a wealthy noble, Crassus, against the awesome slave armies of Spartacus. This leader, a slave from Thrace, had encouraged slaves to follow him to freedom and to their original homelands. After over a year of fighting, Crassus began to get the upper hand; in 71 B.C., he killed Spartacus and defeated the slave army. Pompey, though, returned in time to massacre five thousand slaves and gained for himself a share of the victory.

THE AGE OF AUGUSTUS

These two military lords easily cowed the Senate when it, fearing their power, rejected their request for a triumph and for the consulships for 70 B.C. They were elected. The consuls proceeded, in courting the favor of the Plebeians, to restore the power of veto to the tribunes. Ironically, the Senate now saw reason to fear the ones who were supposed to be pro-Senatorial in sentiments.

At the same time a telling blow was rendered to the Senate's prestige which revealed Senatorial depravity at its worst. A former Governor of Sicily, Verres, had spent three years despoiling the island. Just before his assignment, however, a young lawyer, Cicero, had begun his political career by serving as quaestor in Sicily in 75 B.C. The Sicilians admired Cicero's fairness and honesty, and turned to him for help in prosecuting the greedy Verres. Cicero gathered such damaging evidence so quickly that Verres went into voluntary exile before his case could come to trial. The publication of the case against Verres became a ringing exposition of provincial corruption.

This was the first of many Ciceronian orations to be published. From the fact that Cicero dominated the field of letters from this date until his death, the literary period from 70 B.C. to 43 B.C. is known as the Ciceronian Age of Latin Literature.

Shortly after this two serious problems developed in the East. Rome's lackadaisical policy in policing the shipping lanes had given pirates complete control over the eastern Mediterranean. Roman grain supplies were threatened and her business interests undermined. Again, Mithridates renewed war with Rome when Rome was bequeathed, in a manner similar to the bequest of Pergamum in 133 B.C., the kingdom of Pontus and the King rightly suspected that a closer Roman presence would interfere even more with his realm.

A capable leader, Lucullus, was sent against

Mithridates. He drove Mithridates from his kingdom and captured his capital. But due to his refusal to permit exorbitant interest charges by Roman agents and due to the forbidding plunder by his men, he was attacked viciously at Rome and his army rebelled.

In the meantime, Pompey had been given complete control over suppressing the pirates. When Lucullus had so irritated the business interests by his fair and honest policies that he was forced to retire, his command was transferred to Pompey. Cicero, Praetor in 66 B.C., when this transfer was proposed, spoke heartily in favor of it, hoping thereby to gain Pompey's favor and ultimate support when he, Cicero, was eligible to stand for the consulship for 63 B.C. Pompey was given the command, much to the chagrin of the Senate. On the announcement of the transfer the price of grain immediately dropped, so confident were the business men of Pompey's success.

Pompey had been given absolute power in the East and he began to exercise it. He settled the Pontus problem by forming it into a province. He transformed the kingdom of Armenia into a client kingdom. He abolished the dynasty ruling Syria since Alexander's death and made Syria a province of the Empire. He entered Jerusalem and settled a crisis of leadership among the Jews, paving the way for the rise of Herod the Great in the next generation. He aided the inept ruler of Egypt, Ptolemy the Flute Player, and assured him of Roman backing, thus enabling him to keep his throne. Rome began to hear of more foreign places and strange names than she had ever heard before. She also began to realize that Pompey, upon completing his assignment, could appear in Italy with his army, take over the city and make himself master of Rome and Italy as Sulla had done earlier.

While Pompey was away other leaders tried to advance their cause without his interference. Caesar,

THE AGE OF AUGUSTUS

eager to advance politically, served as Aedile in 65 B.C. In this capacity he gave such extravagant shows and games for the entertainment of the masses that he easily won their favor. When he showed to them that he was sympathetic with Marius's aims—Marius, after all, had been his uncle by marriage—he was assured success. His games, though, bankrupted him. He was forced to work closely with the millionaire Crassus who also wanted to have a bigger voice in state affairs. Together they backed a nobleman, Catiline, for the consulship for the year 63 B.C., confident that he would be a ready accomplice to aid them in their plans.

The conservatives took notice. The aspirations of Caesar were clear and the Senate was alarmed. Because of this, Catiline was defeated in his bid for the highest magistracy and the famous Cicero, as a moderate, was elected instead.

Catiline, irritated at this loss and seeing the support of Caesar and Crassus withdrawn, stood nevertheless as a candidate for consul for the year 62 B.C. Defeated again he then planned to seize the government through a coup d'état, murder the consuls and gain for his economically distressed followers every relief possible.

Cicero ascertained the plot. Catiline's plans were revealed when letters were discovered which gave details of the insurrection. The Consul acted quickly: the ringleaders were executed and Catiline's army, with its leader, was crushed. Cicero was so sure that he had saved the state from a disastrous conflagration that his pride knew no limit. Aside from boasting unceasingly about it for the next twenty years of his life he even wrote an epic poem on the event.

At most the attempted coup revealed that there was a large group of disaffected, debt-ridden aristocrats and farmers who were willing to take extreme measures to achieve their aims.

In the next year, 62 B.C., the victorious Pompey returned from the East. The Senate had already begun to have qualms because of the success and potential power of its erstwhile patron. Its concern was alleviated when Pompey, landing in Italy, disbanded his army; he would not be another Sulla. He appeared simply before the Senate with two requests: ratification of his many settlements in the East and allowances of land for his veterans. In a slap at his prestige, a matter of great importance to Pompey, the Senate rejected both. Caesar, seizing the opportunity, effected an agreement with Pompey. He promised to work for Pompey's requests if Pompey would help him. To obtain additional aid for their cause they brought into their deliberations the wealthy Crassus who was concerned for his financial ventures. The three agreed to take over the state and work for their common interests. Thus the "first triumvirate" was created for the year 60 B.C.

Caesar's plans began to unroll. He realized that he had to have a military arm behind him, and he had none. He desired a consulship and a subsequent provincial command. He was elected consul for the year 59 B.C. He secured Pompey's original requests, and upon completion of his term was given a command for five years in Illyricum (the area of modern Yugoslavia) and Gaul.

With Caesar away, his agent zealously protected his interests in the capital. Pompey's presence in the city seemed to assure his success in maintaining his vested interests. The result was constant strife which, for three years, bordered on mob rule. These personal conflicts suddenly were exacerbated by difficulties with the grain supply. To remedy this the Senate granted Pompey powers to control the grain supply, with proconsular *imperium* over all of the Mediterranean. He quickly solved the problem and, as before, the Senate, fearing his potential power, rebuffed his obvious aim of becoming the undisputed leader of the Empire.

Caesar, meanwhile, was gaining fame, wealth and popularity in his successful conquest of Gaul. Eager to stall any move that would give to Pompey a superior position, Caesar called for a conference of the triumvirs. In 56 B.C. the triumvirate was renewed with each one obtaining his wish: Caesar would remain in Gaul for five additional years; Pompey would rule the wealthy province of Spain; and Crassus would have an army (he now wanted greater military glory) to fight the Parthians who were creating trouble in the area of Syria.

Shortly thereafter the "understanding" began to fray. The mobs continued to roam about the city. Pompey seemed powerless to restrain them. The only powerful link holding Caesar and Pompey together was Julia, Caesar's daughter, who had been given as wife to Pompey. In 54 B.C. she died in childbirth. An affection rarely seen in political marriages had developed between the elderly Pompey and Julia; her demise hastened the rupture with Caesar. Crassus was trapped by the Parthians in the desert area of northern Mesopotamia. He was slain and his army annihilated. The two giants Pompey and Caesar now held the stage to themselves.

So critical had the civil turmoil became in Rome itself that in 52 B.C. the regular elections could not be held. The Senate turned once again to Pompey and created him sole consul for the rest of that year. Pompey was now viewed as the only one capable of restoring order. The Consul himself saw himself as the most important man in the state, the *princeps*—the ranking citizen of the state.

Caesar, anxious about his political fortunes, let it be known that he wanted another year's extension of his command and permission to run for consul *in absentia* while he concluded mopping up operations in Gaul. After lively debate the Senate refused his requests and two of Caesar's agents, the tribunes Antony and Cassius, were expelled. Caesar saw no alternative: he could not, as ordered, disband his army and return to Rome thus unprotected.

He marched so quickly to Rome that, in panic, Pompey and his Senatorial advisors fled to Greece to buy time and to raise an army. Before pursuing them, however, Caesar put Spain under his control when he defeated the Pompeian followers there. He secured his consular election for 48 B.C. and then left for the East. Crossing the Adriatic, unexpectedly, in winter, finally he forced a battle in August of 48 B.C. Pompey was defeated and fled to Egypt where he was confident of aid from the young ruler, the son of the "Flute Player" whom Pompey had befriended fifteen years earlier. As he landed on the shores of Egypt he was met by a royal entourage. Immediately he was beheaded. This Ptolemy preferred the victor, not the vanquished.

Caesar, with his customary dispatch, followed his former son-in-law. Hearing of the ignoble death of a noble Roman, Caesar wept. He put aside the young Ptolemy and made the boy's sister, Cleopatra, the real ruler of Egypt. This charming, alert and capable Macedonian princess was to be in the picture, as a friend of Rome's leaders, for the next eighteen years. With her Caesar remained for a year.

Gradually over the next two years Caesar crushed all opposition and returned to the city at the end of 45 B.C.

The problems facing Caesar were manifold. In massive reforms he began to attempt to resolve them. The class struggle was mitigated by the enrollment of many business men into the Senatorial order. He added provincials to that body as well, making it more representative of the Empire. He reformed the law courts; he increased the number of magistrates to expedite state business; he reduced debts with the wealth from Gaul at his disposal; he planted colonies to ease the growing number of landless veterans and of the masses crowding into the city; he reduced the number of recipients of public grain; he forced the great estates to employ free labor; he brought the calendar up to date, using the knowledge gleaned in Egypt; lastly, he began a beautification program for Rome itself: a library, a new forum, temples, dredging of the Tiber and enlarging of Rome's harbor, Ostia.

As master of the Empire and as one who seemed not to worry about the opinions of others, Caesar's position began to upset several staunch champions of Republican ideals. As one saw his powers and titles one realized that he was absolute. He was Pontifex Maximus, Dictator, Imperator (now granted as an official title), and Pater Patriae; he wore the triumphal laurel leaf constantly, a reminder of his victorious conquests as well as a means to conceal his receding hair line; his divine ancestry, from the goddess Venus, was acknowledged; for the first time in Roman history a leader's portrait, his own, appeared on coins. When in February of 44 B.C. Caesar was proclaimed Dictator for life, his enemies were even more aroused.

For reasons not clearly understood, Caesar, after only six months in the capital, decided to quit Rome for the battlefield. One can speculate that the tasks of the city were tedious to him. He could leave them to his lieutenants. One might think that perhaps he was determined to conquer empires in the East, as he had done in the West, surpassing thereby even Alexander the Great. Regardless of the causes he announced preparations for a campaign against Parthia to avenge Crassus' humiliating defeat and to recover the standards of the legions which were in Parthian hands. On March 15, as he went unguarded to inform the Senate of his plans, he was surrounded and assassinated. A leader of one clique of conspirators was one Brutus, who was consi-

THE AGE OF AUGUSTUS

dered by some to be an illegitimate son of the Dictator.

Immediately two grievous mistakes of the conspirators were revealed: they had no program to offer to implement whatever goals they may have had and they fled the scene, allowing Marc Antony to rally the people against them. As the co-consul for the year with Caesar, Antony quickly took command and seized Caesar's wealth and private papers.

Antony's plans, though, ran into an unexpected trouble. Caesar's will revealed that he had adopted, as his son, the grandson of his sister. This grandnephew, Octavian, had already been sent ahead to Epirus to begin gathering soldiers to join Caesar when the Dictator started toward the East.

Octavian returned to Italy and demanded his inheritance. Antony spurned him. Octavian, on his own, raised money to pay for legacies named in the will and, gradually, veterans of Caesar came over to his side. The elder statesman Cicero saw a golden opportunity to hinder Antony's bid for power: he backed Octavian and encouraged him. Privately, Cicero admitted that as soon as Octavian had served the purpose of blocking Antony, he should be ignored. Urged on by Cicero's vicious attacks on Antony, the Senate finally sent an army against Antony in 43 B.C. The two Consuls were killed in the attacks. Octavian then demanded one of the vacant consulships. This was refused. He was only twenty years old; the minimum age for election was forty-three. Octavian proceeded to capture Rome and forced his election as Consul.

Antony and Octavian now knew they both needed time to recoup and to improve their respective positions. They agreed to work together, and, with another one of Caesar's officers, Lepidus, the Senate was forced to confer upon the three dictatorial powers for five years. Thus, a facade of legality was placed upon this second triumvirate.

THE AGE OF AUGUSTUS

With differences momentarily settled they turned their attention to crushing the conspirators and to exterminating personal opponents in Rome. In Sullan fashion a proscription list was drawn up to do away with enemies and to procure money. Antony demanded the death of Cicero. Octavian was powerless to withstand the request, though he probably would have not attempted to interfere when he realized that Cicero had only planned to use him and, further, he knew that Cicero had hailed the death of his father as "that feast day of the Ides of March." Cicero was captured and beheaded on December 7, 43 B.C.

In 42 B.C. the conspirators were defeated. Octavian and Antony were supreme. The followers of Caesar were victorious. The Republicans were leaderless and powerless.

History soon repeated itself. As Pompey and Caesar had vied for power in the '50s, now Octavian and Antony would do the same.

The triumvirs divided the empire among themselves. Lepidus was given the province of Africa and was made Pontifex Maximus. The taboos of that office and his own vacillating personality rendered him ineffectual as a partner. Octavian took over the West. Antony acquired the East.

Immediately one tried to gain leverage over the other. Antony returned to Italy bent on protecting his interests. As a conflict approached, the two armies refused to fight. In 40 B.C. Octavian and Antony were forced to settle their differences at the seaport town of Brundisium. As a sign of the agreement Octavian's sister, Octavia, was given in marriage to Antony.

A sigh of relief could be felt. Everyone was tiring of fighting, especially veterans who originally were all loyal to Caesar. Such joy was apparent at the peaceful settlement that Virgil, an unabashed admirer of Octavian, wrote an encomium declaring that mankind had entered upon a new age. He likened the new age, in his poetic imagery, to a newborn babe. The early Christian church viewed this as a prophecy of the Messiah. This caused this poem to be called *The Messianic Eclogue* and created a degree of respect from the church for Virgil unknown for other pagan authors.

In the years after this accord Octavian tightened his control over the West and over Italy. In 38 B.C. he married Livia, a matron who would be constantly by his side until his death in 14 A.D. By an earlier marriage Livia had borne two sons, Tiberius and Drusus.

He began to gather around him ministers of the highest quality. Agrippa was his major military advisor but one, also, to whom he would often turn for advice on other matters. Maecenas was the leader of the growing number of literary figures who supported the young Caesar, most notably now Virgil and Horace. Virgil's first published work, the *Eclogues,* had been so successful that Maecenas asked him to compose a work glorifying Italy and emphasizing the love of farming. Virgil worked on this project for seven years; the famous *Georgics* was published in 30 B.C. One can sense that even now Octavian had specific goals and aims in mind, all of which would depend on a peaceful and pacified Italy, the heart of the Empire.

Rome itself was given attention. Under Agrippa's watchful eye building projects were begun: aqueducts, and sewers were built, buildings were repaired.

In 36 B.C. Octavian's political posture was strengthened by the grant which made his person "sacred." With his proconsular rank and the authority of the triumvirate which had been renewed the year before, his legal position was sufficient. Nevertheless, he desired to be elected consul for the second time in 33 B.C. Achieving this, now at the age of 30, the onus of his having held his first consulship at the age of 20 was somewhat removed.

Antony, meanwhile, was governing the East, with Octavia at his side, from Athens. In discharging his duties Cleopatra of Egypt once again came into the picture.

The Queen, in seeking what was best for Egypt, realized that she had to work with Rome to obtain anything. She had made Egypt an ally of Rome and had wielded considerable influence with Caesar. With his premature death she now turned to the warlord of the East, Antony.

Antony knew that Egypt's vast resources could aid him in his plans to subdue Parthia. This had been Caesar's dream and now it was a venture for which he was preparing. He came, though, completely under Cleopatra's charm, intrigued by her wit, her knowledge of languages and her dreams of restoring Egypt to the days of pharaonic glory. When he started out on the Parthian expedition he sent his wife Octavia back to Rome and openly married Cleopatra. The campaign was unsuccessful; his army was barely saved from destruction.

In this turn of events Octavian was given ample propanganda fuel. His attacks on his colleague became stronger when Antony gave several eastern provinces to Cleopatra and her children, a right he legally possessed, since they all would still be ruled on Rome's behalf. Octavian, though, inveighed only against the Queen, carefully avoiding the appearance of fomenting another civil war. When war was declared it was against Egypt, not Antony.

War broke out in the spring of 31 B.C. At the site of **Actium**, in Western Greece, a naval battle occurred on September 2 of that year. Cleopatra, unexpectedly and with her treasure, abandoned the fight. Antony followed her, deserting his men and his fleet.

The army of Antony went over to Octavian. With no one now to question his military supremacy the young Caesar consolidated his hold over Asia Minor, Syria and

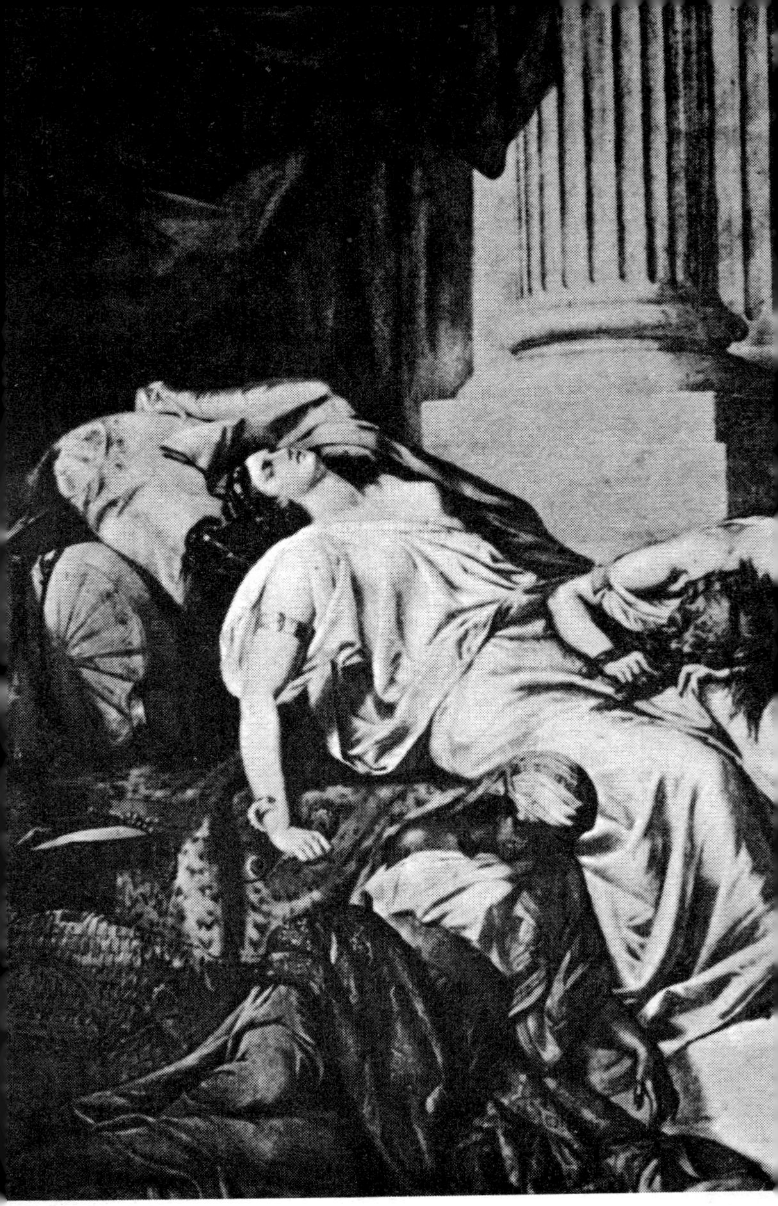

Augustus and Cleopatra

Palestine and marched into Egypt the next year. Antony and Cleopatra committed suicide. The newly designated ruler of Egypt, Gallus, ruling as the representative of Octavian, crushed a rebellion in southern Egypt, a center of Egyptian nationalism, and wiped out all opposition to Roman control.

With the wealth of the Ptolemies at his command Octavian returned to Rome in 29 B.C., and celebrated three days of magnificent triumphal marches. Before his chariot walked nine kings or children of kings. He settled his army without disturbing confiscations and began to give his attention to other matters. The Empire now awaited the will of the victor. Octavian at the age of thirty-four years held a power equalled in history only by that of Alexander the Great and Julius Caesar.

The days of a government by "the Senate and the Roman people" were over. The Mediterranean world would now look toward the age of the Caesars.

Now, though, there was peace, an unquestioned peace, for the first time in over one hundred years.

Octavian still held his triumviral powers approved for the Second Triumvirate. This was primarily a military position, one which now seemed less and less desirable because of the lack of any military opposition. Eager now not to be considered a military dictator in the eyes of the Romans, as Sulla and Caesar had been, he felt it was imperative that his official status be clarified.

In January of 27 B.C. one of the most intriguing series of conversations in ancient history, left unrecorded for us, must have taken place. Octavian announced that he was resigning all of his extraordinary powers. The Senate, made up of his loyal supporters, most assuredly was shaken by the awareness that a void would suddenly be created by such a step that could precipitate an unthinkable crisis. The veterans and the legions of the Empire all now looked to Caesar's heir as their

Imperator; a sudden retirement by Octavian could permit ambitious soldiers to pursue careers reminiscent of Marius and Sulla. Political and military chaos could ensue.

The Senate begged Octavian to reconsider. An accommodation, they must have said, could be reached whereby he could still share in the government. After all, no one in the Mediterranean world could approach Octavian with a comparable record of military achievements. No one could compare himself to the young Caesar's other personal achievements, most notably avenging his father's assassination, completing the building of temples, aqueducts and sewers, holding the tribunician privileges and the incumbent sacrosanctity. In short the "influence" of Octavian surpassed all in every realm of activity. The Romans referred to this simply and inimitably: his *auctoritas* surpassed all others, and he was only 36 years old.

Of these facts Octavian himself was most aware. Yet the question of his status had to be resolved, with no implication of military force or threat. Whether or not his handling of this situation was through guile or sincerity on his part, the result surely was what he wanted: he was to receive from the Senate and Roman people newly conferred powers, powers given at a time of peace, not as a result of military crises. He could then announce that he had "restored the Republic" and that he had returned the state from his "own power to that of the Senate and People."

Cautiously he felt his way. He had to keep control over the army. To this end he received and accepted supreme command, or *imperium,* over the provinces in which standing armies were required. These became technically the imperial provinces. In those provinces which required little, if any, military presence he saw to it that the traditional Senatorial supervision was imposed. By virtue of this arrangement he was given military ascendency with no emotional nuances of "king" or "dictator." For the moment this was sufficient.

Other latent powers, nevertheless, were at his disposal. He had been one of the two consuls consecutively since 31 B.C. His influence over other ex-magistrates was so unlimited that he could easily control governors and magistrates in any province, even in the Senatorial ones. His personal wealth and income was virtually equal to the Empire's entire income. With this he could dispose of any problem requiring financial attention: securing the grain supply, building roads, providing spectacles for the masses and remodeling or erecting new public buildings and temples. Most notably there was another unique factor in the area of his *auctoritas:* he was the "son of the deified Julius." The aura of this mystic title was increased by a Senatorial decree granting to Octavian the majestic title of "Augustus," "Revered One" or "One of Good Omen." Formally, however, he preferred the title *Princeps,* a title not only meaning "First Gentleman of the State," but also conveying a mark of deference to Republican tradition. At no time had he failed to abide by precedents already established. Extended *imperium* had been given to Sulla and Pompey. The Gracchi brothers and Marius had held offices consecutively. The tribunician privileges had been used for the forwarding of programs deemed necessary for the public good. The only innovations were his titles, the mystic aura of his "deified" father and his incomparable *auctoritas.*

While our information for the next three or four years is scanty, they were years which presented new problems to the Emperor.

In 27 B.C. trouble developed in Spain. For three years the Prince led campaigns in northwestern Spain. The strenuous work proved debilitating; his health appeared more and more precarious. He was taken ill and had to recuperate in 25 B.C.

His weak health constantly provoked the question of what would happen if he were taken from the scene. The Emperor seems to have felt that only someone closely related and akin to him could survive such a crisis and keep the state on an even keel. Though he must have given thought to Rome's willingness to accept such a dynastic solution, he nevertheless set such a plan in motion.

His only child, his daughter Julia, was married in 25 B.C. to Marcellus, the son of Augustus' sister Octavia. Julia was fourteen years old, Marcellus eighteen. This alliance obviously marked Marcellus as the successor-designate to the Emperor. He was bound by blood and marriage to the Prince. The imperial favor was further shown by the authorization of the Senate that Marcellus could stand for the consulship ten years before the age required by law.

Tragically, Marcellus died unexpectedly two years later. The youth was immediately immortalized by the poet Virgil in Book VI of his opic poem, the *Aeneid*, which he now was composing. For Augustus this would be the first of many tragedies that would plague his attempts to groom a successor. Shortly thereafter Julia was married to the trusted lieutenant Agrippa.

Ominous news came from Egypt in 26 B.C. Gallus, the Viceroy, had erected a monument to his own glory after considerable success in military operations in Ethiopia. Such a monument or display could not be allowed to the Emperor's representative. It slighted the person of the Emperor, and also revived fears of a revival of ambitious generals. Gallus was summoned to Rome and, in disgrace, committed suicide.

Augustus returned to Rome from Spain in 24 B.C. In the next year his delicate health again was revealed: he was taken grievously ill and was on the verge of death. He was saved only when his physician applied cold treatments which corrected what seems to have been a case of typhoid fever.

In the same year another shock came to the Emperor. His colleague as co-consul for the year was found to be guilty of conspiracy against him. The conspiracy was crushed and the leaders were executed.

The awareness that there were groups who were capable of plotting against him forced the Prince to take vigorous action.

Part of the restlessness revealed in the nobilty was caused by the fact that Augustus had seen fit to hold one of the two consulships consecutively since 31 B.C. This magistracy he had thought important with its powers of convening the Senate and of introducing business. But by holding one of the two offices he was creating an embarrassing situation for his supposed "colleague" and he was depriving others from obtaining the office that was the highest in the political ladder and provided one of the main keys, as ex-consul, for gubernatorial assignments in the provinces.

On July 1, he resigned the consulship, summoned the Senate and carefully legalized the new steps he deemed necessary.

The cornerstone of his new power was the traditional *imperium*. This was always a consular prerogative and as an ex-consul, or proconsul, this was the source for the absolute power of a Roman governor. Since, though, he now has resigned his consular position he, technically, could exercise proconsular *imperium* which was valid both in the city and in all provinces. The authority granted by this settlement was staggering: he was the ultimate authority in the Roman world, the troops took their military oath in his name, he decided on the allocation of all public lands, he was the origin of all honors, he could declare war or make peace and he could interpose his will in all affairs, in all of the Senatorial provinces of the empire.

The *maius imperium* easily provided the answers for

THE AGE OF AUGUSTUS

problems arising outside of Rome itself. Within the inner workings of the government of the Republic, however, the tribunician power had been the key to the control of legislation and of magistrates. He was now granted tribunician power without the obligation of holding the office.

These grants, the *imperium* and the tribunician power made Augustus all powerful in the military, legislative and provincial realm. These powers and his *auctoritas* gave him control over nominations for all offices including the priesthoods. The only office of significance he did not now hold was that of Pontifex Maximus. He would wait until the death of Lepidus ten years later to assume that position.

Secure now in his position, the Emperor could embark on other programs.

The East required attention. He sent his step-son Tiberius and Agrippa to resolve provincial problems. The Parthian danger was still present; Herod the Great was eager to make his kingdom loyal to Rome; the borders of other client states had to be fixed. The diplomatic success of Tiberius and Agrippa permitted the Emperor to take a leisurely tour of these areas between 22 and 19 B.C.

He journeyed via Sicily and Greece, creating new colonies as he went. He visited Athens and the islands of the Aegean. Coming to the area of Parthia he concluded an agreement with its king whereby the sacred military standards of Crassus' army were restored to Rome and the Euphrates river was acknowledged as the border of the two empires.

To show that Rome was equal in architectural accomplishments to the Hellenistic monarchs who ruled Syria until Pompey's conquest, Augustus established a military colony at the modern site of Baalbeck. Here still stand the most imposing temple ruins of Rome's imperial period.

THE AGE OF AUGUSTUS

For two years after his return to Rome in 19 B.C. the Emperor initiated a series of moral legislative reforms. He made adultery a criminal offense. He enacted laws against childless marriages. He forbade luxury and tried to regulate the number of slaves who might be freed and given citizenship. In such regulations as these Augustus was to be generally unsuccessful. He would find, as others before and after him have found, that it is difficult to legislate the morals of a society.

In 17 B.C. his government, now referred to as the Principate, from *Princeps*, had lasted for ten years. In every major area of social, political and military activity the Empire seemed to be at peace. The Emperor decided to have an elaborate, impressive religious ceremony to mark the year, and to promulgate a re-dedication and a rejuvenation of mankind. A comet appeared to give divine blessing to his plan. For three days elaborate sacrifices and prayers were made to specific deities. The poet Horace created the hymn which twenty-seven young boys and twenty-seven young girls sang in honor of Apollo and Diana.

The Romans, now victorious and now purified, were prepared to enter into a new historical cycle.

In the following year the Emperor began his last provincial tour, this time going to the western provinces. He gave much attention to Gaul, an area which history was to reveal as perhaps one of the most Romanized provinces of the Empire. Road systems were projected, the government was streamlined and an imperial mint was built there. Spain, too, was organized and the affinity of modern Spanish to Latin attests to the Romanization of that province.

The solution to a vexing problem was to elude Augustus. The northern borders would continue for centuries to be a matter of concern to the Empire. The Emperor attempted, though, to establish a natural, defendible northern frontier. A natural line would be the flow of the Rhine and Danube Rivers. This border is long, over seven hundred miles, and thought was given to pushing Roman power more to the north to create a line along the Elbe River to the Danube. This would be only five hundred miles in length. A German campaign was begun by Drusus, the Emperor's stepson, whom he considered his best commander. In 9 B.C. Drusus died as a result of an accident and his aims were not realized.

For two more decades the Roman legions would fight in this northern area. Tiberius led the armies in the province of Illyricum, the area where the Danube comes close to the Adriatic Sea. There a rebellion developed that took three years to repress. In the year of the quelling of this revolt, 9 A.D., another favorite general, Varus, led his legions into the western borders of modern Germany. He met with disaster. His army was annihilated and he committed suicide. Augustus, now seventy-two and viewing these military ventures with alarm, was for weeks in a state of semi-mourning, wailing for the return of his lost legions.

The plan of a Danube-Rhine border was to be the one adopted. The Emperor could no longer continue to keep the majority of his military forces engaged in a fruitless attempt to extend the Empire, and the Danube borders had to be protected. So concerned was Augustus that this settlement be accepted he enjoined his successor not to alter this policy.

During the long period of Augustus' rule three matters of prime importance for future years were cared for: the civil service, the army and the city.

No Empire can function without the day-to-day care of its business. A civil service was organized and Augustus urged that men of ability be chosen to serve the state. A great improvement resulted in the government of provinces when the terms of office were extended for conscientious and capable governors. Collection of taxes was now done on a fair and equitable basis, aided by regular census returns. Under Augustus no Verres could appear.

The Roman armies became a professional corps. In a long period of service the Emperor encouraged one of the positive points in Marius' reforms. He allowed a service of sixteen years, and upon discharge the legionary soldier received a pension. Such sureties easily created a dedicated soldiery. Each legion was commanded by a nominee of the Emperor. The men took an oath to the Emperor as their commander-in-chief. Archeological evidence and Roman writers point to the pride evoked by achievements of individual legions.

Much needed to be done to improve the capital city. The government of the Republic, by its nature, precluded any major, logical development program. Such plans can be carried out only over an extended period of time, under steady guidance and financing. Except for Julius Caesar no one had had an opportunity to proceed with any grand plan until the age of Augustus. The fact that he undertook projects before Actium has been noted. During the long term of his reign eighty-two temples were built or remodeled. The Forum of Julius was finished and one named for the Emperor was built. Libraries were attached to the great temple of Apollo, Augustus' patron deity. The Senate House was rebuilt. A new theater, in honor of Marcellus, was constructed. Agrippa himself supervised the construction of a temple to the "All-divine One," the Pantheon, which still stands with later modifications.

Both in its artistry and in its significance, the most striking monument erected by the Emperor was his Altar of Peace, constructed between 13 and 9 B.C. It was decorated with exquisite symbols of Rome's founding, of her present prosperity and of the peace Augustus had wrought. A magnificent processional relief was executed portraying the important figures of the time coming to the altar to do homage. Here one can see, among many others, Augustus, Livia, Agrippa, Julia and Virgil.

The Emperor was determined that Rome appear to be worthy of her imperial role. While later he would boast, somewhat incorrectly, that he had found Rome to be a city of brick and had transformed it into a city of marble, he did achieve the goal of elevating Rome architecturally to a level more comparable to the grand, well-planned Hellenistic city-states.

Other measures improved the day-to-day life of the citizens of the city. His personal body guard, the famous Praetorian Guard, was created to protect him and to aid in the policing of the city. The city was divided into fourteen districts with a fire force and a police corps in each. He created a Board of Public Works to maintain the public structures and to enforce new regulations, one of which limited the height of new structures to sixty feet. He felt, though wrongly, that this might relieve congestion, since many apartment houses had originally been built higher. These buildings tended to become slum pockets for the landless and fire raps for the inhabitants.

In the actual governing of the city and Empire he was aided and advised by a select committee composed of the consuls, representatives from the other magistracies and private individuals chosen by lot. Shortly before his death members of the imperial family were added. He had, in addition, informal meetings with an advisory committee of judges and assessors. The two groups prepared the way for the development of the "Advisory Committee of the Emperor," a group that would become more and more important in imperial history.

In no area of activity was Augustus more successful than in his attempts to create a new spiritual attitude and intellectual horizon for his people. His reign was

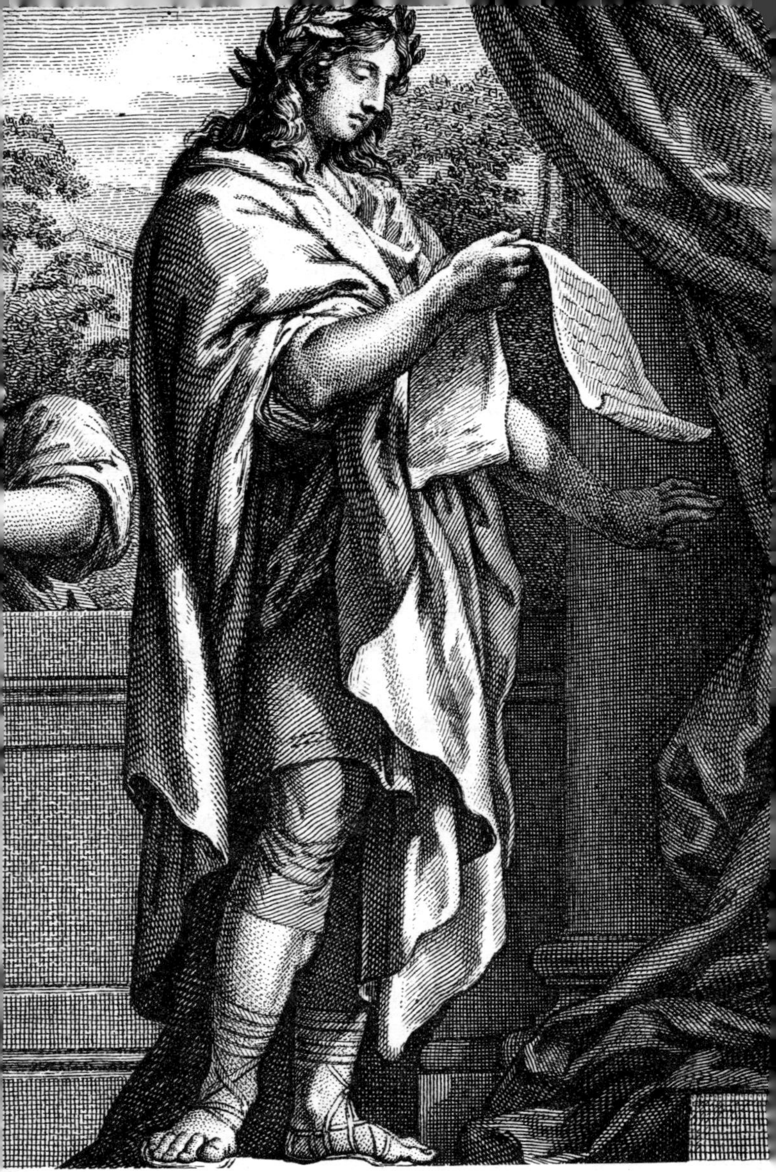

Virgil and Augustus

long enough to instill and to sustain new ideas, and to rejuvenate Roman pride in her many accomplishments.

The Emperor was determined to present himself and his era as one ordained by Heaven to bring human events into a proper, rational order. It was with divine sanction that Romans were an imperial people and it was with the special blessing of the gods that the family of Caesar had achieved the pinnacle of power. But, just as important, Augustus was eager to demonstrate that the awesome successes of Rome were the logical unrolling of events that followed closely upon two other eras of inimitable human achievement, the Hellenic and Hellenistic ages. He wanted a clear link established with the past, demonstrating his belief that, in this, Rome could see herself in a proper perspective. But more too: not only did he want Rome to understand that she was the natural heir to past accomplishments, he wanted Rome to see that she was rightful preserver and transmitter of these earlier ages.

Nor could the Emperor himself help but attain a mystical position in the collective mind of the Empire. His *auctoritas* was enhanced with every passing year. The title "Augustus," given so early in his reign, seemed more and more an appropriate one in that he was "one of good omen." A citizen of this age could hardly doubt that he was uniquely endowed with a supernatural aura. At a time when it was natural for one to stand in awe of those who accomplished the seemingly impossible, it was a simple step for one to pay veneration to the guiding spirit of that personality. Hence, Augustus' "genius," as the spirit was called, became an object of worship.

This is the background for the future worship of the Roman Emperor as the head and the personification of the Roman state, the state which florished or floundered according to the wisdom of the Prince.

In these thoughts Maecenas and his circle of literary

THE AGE OF AUGUSTUS

figures also played a leading role. The masterpieces of literature created at this time ring with the themes of a consciousness of pride and purpose, and of praises for the Emperor.

The great epic of the Augustan Age, Virgil's *Aeneid*, has as its main theme the escape of Aeneas from the flames of Troy and, under divine auspices, the establishment of the Trojan remnant in Italy. All of this served two purposes: to found, ultimately, a new Troy, Rome; and to restore a balance to human affairs which is seen when these future Trojans, now Romans, in turn conquer Greece. Virgil pictures Jupiter as declaring that this is the decree of the Fates, and that, when these events are accomplished, there will be no temporal or spiritual limits to a future ruler, another "Aeneas"—Augustus himself.

Horace, the lyric genius of the day, would create such beautiful poetry that he could make the claim that he had brought the lyric muse of Greek poetry to Rome. He does not hesitate to exclaim that Augustus Caesar is the Vice-Regent of Jupiter on earth, nor does he miss a chance to extol the simple virtues of frugality, peace of mind and old Roman morality. Livy, the "ivory tower scholar," will for almost fifty years write his monumental history of Rome. He, too, will seize every opportunity to demonstrate the value of the old morality as he describes the many virtues attributed to the mighty personalities of Rome's early Republican heroes.

Each of these literary themes provided a link to the past, a goal for the present and a hope for the future.

Perhaps further, one might add, in pursuing these goals Augustus appears as modern as many leaders viewed on the stage of history today. Who has not heard of the call to personal and national service? Who has not heard of a desire to return to the proven values of the past? Who is not aware of the need to build for the future? We are not far removed in thought from this person separated by two millenia from us.

The last years of Augustus were years that can best be described as ones of anguish for the future. Now that he had restored the state it was imperative that the newly created order be peacefully transmitted to a successor. We have seen that earlier he felt only a relative could secure this. These attempts had proved to be unsuccessful; so would subsequent attempts. Marcellus had died. Agrippa, designated as the successor who would hand the state ultimately to one of his sons, the Emperor's grandsons, died in 12 B.C. The grandsons, Lucius and Gaius, in whom were the greatest of hopes, were in turn advanced in rank and were presented as undoubted heirs. The former died in 2 A.D. at the age of fifteen, the latter in 4 A.D. at sixteen.

The Emperor now had no alternative. In the year of Gaius' death he adopted his step-son, Tiberius, as his son. In spite of a lack of affection between the two, Tiberius had demonstrated military astuteness and abilities in leadership. After Agrippa's death he had been selected as tutor for Lucius and Gaius, and had been required, in 11 B.C., to marry the hand-me-down, widowed Julia as a sign of close association with the Emperor. The marriage was distasteful to Tiberius, who later retired to Rhodes. This withdrawal was the probable cause of a rift between the Emperor and his son. Upon the occasion of the adoption Augustus declared, coldly, that it was for the "good of the state."

Tiberius earlier had been granted the tribunician power. In 13 A.D. he was given this power again for ten years and was granted proconsular *imperium* equal to that of Augustus. His orderly succession to the supreme position was assured. When Augustus died the following year Tiberius assumed the purple as expected.

While much is known about his accomplishments,

the personal life and character of the Emperor is difficult to capture. Random comments by biographers give hints and clues. He was simple in his tastes and habits. He preferred the clothes woven by his wife to other sumptuous garments. His living quarters were simple. It was his successors who built palaces. He was generous to friends and expected those close to him to adhere to his standards. He was within character when he banished his daughter and granddaughter for their immorality.

He gave inordinate attention to the common, day-to-day affairs of men. Authors commented on this trait. Such concern elicited the desired reaction, the affection of his people. When, in 2 B.C., he received the title "Father of his Country" he exclaimed that it was the most significant honor he had received. Another touching scene evidences this concern of his and, in an unusual way, reveals popular reaction. A few days before he died he was returning to Rome after a tour near Naples. He stopped for a rest near the Port of Puteoli (where St. Paul would later land in Italy). As it happened a grain ship en route from Egypt was also there. On learning that the Emperor was there the crew, dressed in white, greeted him with garlands and incense. They praised him for enabling them to sail peacefully and for preserving their lives and occupations. He rewarded each with forty pieces of gold.

His government was careful but firm. His favorite advice was to make haste slowly. This reflected a policy of patience rather than one of adventure. This is seen in his dealings with Parthia, in his refusal to permit military moves in Germany and, most clearly, in the studied accumulation of his personal powers. His methodical and careful ways are well reflected in the fact that he noted on every letter the exact hour of the day or night on which he had composed it.

His aims, and even the means employed, reflect his simple origin in the Latium town of Velitrae, a few miles away from the Appian Way. He was brought up by his mother since his father died when he was four years old. At an early age he was introduced to life in Rome by Julius Caesar himself. One can easily imagine the contrast the future Prince saw between life in the country town and life in the capital.

In his formative years every opportunity presented itself to encourage those qualities that were with him until he died: self-command and self-confidence, patience, and a remarkable judgment of facts and personalities. As he struggled to correct the national ills, while holding a personal dedication to avenge his father, these traits were his salvation. He dealt astutely with Antony, Cicero, Caesar's legions, Cleopatra, the conspirators, the Senate, the die-hard Republicans and foreign leaders who were allied to Rome.

His monumental creation, a new form of government, had its faults. Too many administrative responsibilities were placed upon his successors, many of whom were not equal to the task. Yet it is a marvel that there were not more!

The northern borders of the Empire remained static. Centuries later they would crack.

Thousands of the populace were downtrodden. Later they would seek aid from ambitious generals, repeating the cancerous days of the Republic. Or they would turn to new faiths when the genius of the Emperor or the might of the Empire offered no security. One such faith, Christianity, born under Augustus, would ultimately, however, preserve the spirit of the Empire.

Any civilization, though, is always a matter of careful and considered compromises. This Augustus fully appreciated. That the answer to the many problems which debilitated the Republic required the "compromise" of an absolute executive seems to admit no argument. The positive results of his settlement attest to this.

For the first time in memory there was a viable, meaningful peace. A famous author of the next generation, Pliny the Elder, aptly coined the phrase describing it as "the immense majesty of the Roman Peace."

Trade and commerce flourished. Industry was revived in Italy and in the provinces. The provinces were administered with reason and concern.

Old national boundaries were meaningless. One could travel from Gaul to Palestine, from Numidia to Macedonia safely and without impediment. Without this the early Christian movement would not have left Palestine.

Two languages, Greek and Latin, became universal. New ideas and thoughts could easily be interchanged.

Areas that only decades before had been considered barbarian were brought the blessings, admittedly for some at a costly price, of Roman civilization.

For centuries to come, Europe would dream of this period. During the dark and chaotic era of the Middle Ages civilized man would long for the peace and stability of the Roman Empire. Kings and emperors would emulate their earlier Roman prototype. There would be for centuries the august title of "Holy Roman Emperor" conjuring up the majestic link to the past.

That one man created for, and in, his own day a new way of life is unusual. That this creation would excite the imagination of untold future generations is an achievement reserved for few.

Several days after the Emperor was hailed by the crew of the grain ship, he was aware that life was ebbing. Weak and exhausted, lying on his bed, he summoned the strength to compose himself. He straightened his hair and summoned his devoted wife Livia, the last person left on earth for him to love, to his arms. His last words to her were, "In the comedy of life have I played my part well?"

There can be only one answer.

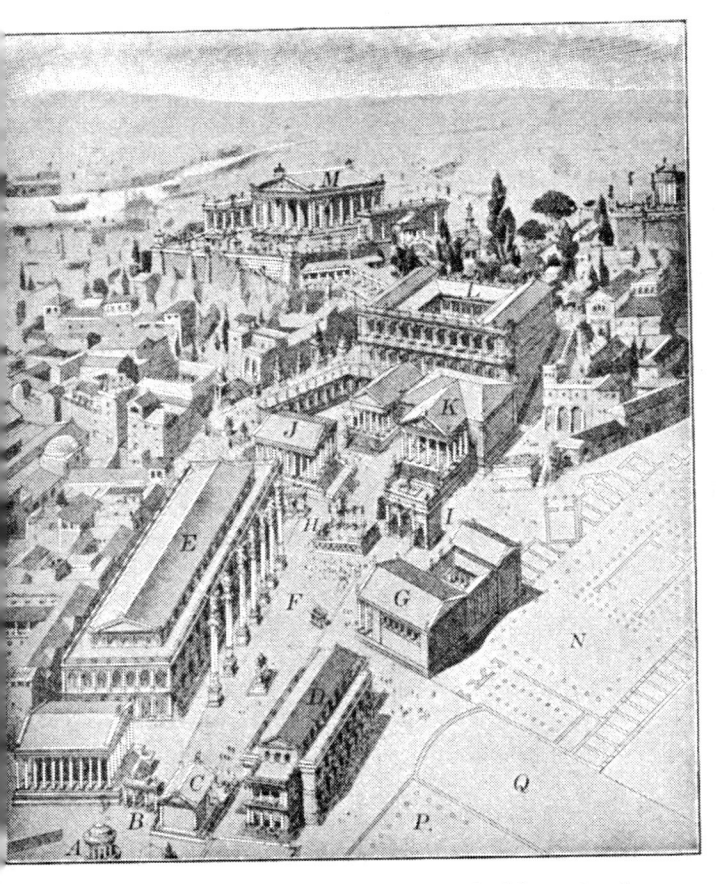

The Roman Forum and its public buildings in the early Empire

AN ARCHITECT FOR ALL AGES

By Richard J. Hunter

A modern man walking leisurely along the East River in Manhattan or approaching the city of New York in a plane from the sky sees extending hopefully out of the hard rock of Manhattan a twentieth century architectural structure overwhelming in its simplicity and beauty, a shimmering jewel of glass and steel—the United Nations Building.

Our same man seeing a Mies van der Rohe apartment building on the Chicago Lake front, or Frank Lloyd Wright's Price Tower springing from the stark flat prairie, or Walter Gropius' Bauhaus in Dessau, Germany, or Corbusier's Savoye House at Poissy is immediately aware that he is looking at forms of the "new" living architecture of today—up-to-date structures utilizing modern materials and technologies all enveloping modern life.

And our same man is acutely aware that these buildings represent universal social concepts of man's life *today*—for architecture, unlike painting or sculpture which can be housed in museums, cannot survive independent of the people and the machines which serve them. Only in its briefest phases can architecture express the thoughts and feelings of an individual. Architecture, unlike music, is not an introspective art. It does not lend itself readily to self-expression. What emotional relationships architecture established are those of men in group associations; its meanings are relevant to individuals chiefly as these participate in the life of society. Its main concerns are philosophy, government—the life of men together.

In the United Nations Building, for example, a man upon entering inherently knows that the building is a living embodiment of the hope of twentieth century man to establish a fraternal organization of universal scope to allow all men of all races to live honorably in a complex society which holds more weapons for the ultimate destruction of the world than ever before known. He knows, too, that he is also a living part of that building and its intent.

But our modern man, seeing modern buildings enveloping modern philosophy constructed of modern materials by means of modern technology, would be somewhat reduced in ego if he were cognizant of how much of what is regarded as "new," "modern," "international," "contemporary" architecture was conceived in the mind and writings of a man who lived nearly 2,000 years ago. This man, for the Roman Emperor Octavius (Caesar) Augustus who "found Rome a city of clay and left it a city of marble," wrote ten books, *De Architectura*, in which he laid down principles of architecture still essential today—principles as solid and as pertinent to modern architecture as the Ten Commandments are to religious thought, law, and order.

AN ARCHITECT FOR ALL AGES

The author of *De Architectura* was an architect and an engineer, Marcus Vitruvius Pollio, who it is believed was born in the city Mola di Gaeta somewhere between 83 and 73 B.C. When he was introduced to Caesar Augustus by the Emperor's beloved sister Octavia, Vitruvius was "bowed with age," of low stature, and suffering from poor health. He had been an engineer in the army of the great Gaius Julius Caesar during the Gallic Wars where he had undoubtedly acquired a great deal of his knowledge in the actual building of roads, bridges, and military fortifications.

He probably became acquainted with Octavia during her marriage to Mark Anthony, and following her divorce when her brother was proclaimed "Princeps" in 27 B.C., Vitruvius under the Emperor's sponsorship began his architectural manuscript. He dedicated his work to the Emperor and his influence is apparent in the finest work of the Augustan Age of classical Roman architecture. Of Vitruvius' own architectural work, there is but a single building that can actually be attributed to him—the basilica at Fanum Fortunae, now known as Fano, Italy.

Vitruvius was a visionary; when he took upon himself the task of writing the history and the objectives of architecture for Augustus, he wrote: "When I saw that you were giving your attention not only to the welfare of society in general and to the establishment of the public order, but also to providing public buildings intended for utilitarian purposes, so that the State would not only be enriched with provinces by your means, but that the greatness of its power might likewise be attended with distinguished authority in its public buildings, I thought I ought to take the first opportunity to lay before you my writings on this theme."

From these writings we learn what we know of the man, Vitruvius. We learn that he was not wealthy and that wealth held little importance for him, since he considered the pursuit of knowledge and the development and application of his thoughts to the advancement of society and culture far more important than the acquisition of money. He writes, "I have acquired intellectual possessions whose chief fruits are these thoughts: that superfluity is useless, and that not to feel the want of anything is true riches."

Vitruvius reveals himself as a man of high principle and dedication, a purist insofar as his ideas on art and architecture are concerned. To his ideals he made no compromises. As he walked through the streets of Rome, over the bridges, under the triumphal arches, he must have been deeply concerned as he saw example after example of crudely applied and poorly proportioned Greek forms and details. Having spent many years of travel and study in Greece, he was accepted as an authority on Hellenistic philosophy, science, and architecture. He regarded knowledge and education as providing lasting values for mankind. "All the gifts which fortune bestows she can easily take away, but education when combined with intelligence never fails, but abides steadily on to the very end of life."

In writing his *De Architectura*, Vitruvius intended to run the gamut of architectural knowledge for others to study and practice. He included philosophy, knowledge of the arts and sciences and the practical training of architects, information on specific construction methods, and the description and uses of known materials. He established principles of proportion, arrangement, and design and described in extensive detail Greek buildings which he classified in *Orders,* outlining their historical development. Until Vitruvius' books the only record the world had of Greek architecture was the writings of the poet Homer, who described life and culture of the Mycenaean Age without any specifics to give an understanding of the art and techniques employed by Greek architects.

The ten books are each relatively short and concise.

To Augustus, Vitruvius explains that he has done this purposely because writing on the subject of architecture is not like writing history or poetry, both these subjects being more captivating for the reader and less tedious. He also states that he has observed "Our citizens are distracted with public affairs and private business," and, therefore, without the leisure to read and comprehend lengthy treatises.

Book I deals with the education of an architect and the basic principles of architecture. Vitruvius discusses city sites, city streets (orienting them with the winds), and sites for public buildings. In Book II he tells his own story of the origin of the dwelling and uses his own travels throughout Greece and Gaul to show how man's dwelling logically evolved with his environment, relating to the natural landscapes and being built out of available materials. In Book III and Book IV he details the history of Greek architecture.

Book V is concerned with public buildings, where they should be placed and how they should be designed. He discusses forums, basilicas, baths, the treasury, prisons and even gives suggestions for harbors, breakwaters, and shipyards. In Book VI he deals with the private residence in the determination of a style relating it to its climate and modifying the design to suit the site, and gives instructions to the proper proportions of the rooms to suit the occupant. In Book VII he discusses the construction of floors and gives detailed information on how to manufacture stucco, vault ceilings, and plaster damp rooms successfully. He also discusses painting and the use of colors and marbles.

Of color he says: "The fact is that the artistic excellence which the Ancients (Greeks) endeavored to attain by working hard and taking pains is now attempted by the use of colors and the brave show they make and expenditure by the employer prevents people from missing the artistic refinements which once lent authority to works. For example, which of the Ancients can have been found to have used vermillion otherwise than sparingly, like a drug? But today whole walls are covered with it everywhere. Then, too, there was malachite green, purple, and Armenian blue. When these colors are laid on, they present a brilliant appearance to the eye, even though they are inartistically applied; and, as they are costly, they are made exceptions in contracts, to be furnished by the employer not by the contractor."

(This statement has a familiar ring today when we often see displays of tasteless, garish cacophonies of color employed solely, it appears, to shock the observer and dull his senses.)

Book VIII propounds the various means of finding water and the distribution of water through aqueducts and pipes and analyzes cistern construction and the manufacture and use of leveling instruments. In Book IX Vitruvius investigates the then familiar sciences and includes an outline of known astronomy, a discourse on the moon and the zodiac, and the rules for building sundials and water clocks. In Book X Vitruvius tabulates specific machines and implements and their structure, such as machines for raising water, for measuring the speed of ships, and military machines for hurling missiles and maintaining defenses.

For Augustus, for the architect, and for the reader, Vitruvius defines his theme of the fundamental principles of architecture: "Architecture depends upon Order, Arrangement, Eurythmy, Symmetry, Propriety and Economy." He explains that Order gives due measure to the parts of a work considered separately and symmetrical agreement to the proportions of the whole. "By this," he writes, "I mean the selection of the modules from the members of the work itself, and starting from these individual parts of members constructing the whole work to correspond."

AN ARCHITECT FOR ALL AGES

"Arrangement includes the putting of things into their proper places . . . the elegance of the effect [is a result of] adjusting these elements of the plan to be appropriate to the character of the particular project." Eurythmy he defines as "beauty and fitness in the adjustment of the members. This is found when the members of the work are of a height suited to their breadth, of a breadth suited to their length, and in a word, they all correspond symmetrically."

Symmetry is "a proper agreement between the members of the work itself, and the relation between the different parts and the whole general scheme in accordance with a certain part selected as standard." For an analogy he points to the human body, "in which there is a kind of symmetrical harmony between the forearm, foot, palm, finger, and all other small parts; so it is with a perfect building."

Propriety, we learn, is "that perfection of style which comes when a work is authoritatively constructed on approved principles. It arises from usage when buildings having magnificent interiors are provided with elegant entrance courts to correspond, for there would be no propriety to the spectacle of an elegant interior approached by a low, mean entrance." And Economy, he explains, "involves the proper management of materials and of site, as well as a thrifty balance of costs and common sense in the construction of works."

How modern is the thinking of this man who lived in the first century B.C., Dr. Walter Gropius in *The New Architecture in the Bauhaus* states: "The modern building should derive its architectural significance from the vigor and consequence of its own organic proportions. It must be true to itself, logically transparent, and virginal of lies and trivialities as befits direct approbation of our contemporary world of mechanization and rapid transit."

Le Corbusier has remarked: ". . . when an architec-

161

ture is genuinely appropriate to its environment it gives a pleasing sensation of harmony and is profoundly moving." And Frank Lloyd Wright wrote: "Form and function become one in design and execution when the nature of materials and method and purpose are all in unison. In any final result there can be no separation between our architecture and our culture, nor any separation of either from our happiness, nor any separation from our work."

Thus the leading thought in modern design corroborates the ancient text of Vitruvius and decrees that the aesthetic form of structure must by existing within its own space-time relationships be the end result of practical, logical developments of its special conditions and use.

The ten books of *De Architectura* were lost for many centuries after the Augustan Age, but they were rediscovered in the fifteenth century at St. Gall. The oldest existing manuscript dates from about the tenth century. The first edition was printed in Latin in Rome in 1486, just after Gutenberg's invention of the moving printing press. In 1496 and 1497 eleven more editions appeared in Latin. During the sixteenth century there were two copies in French, two in German, and seven in Latin.

One of the most famous manuscripts of Vitruvius was the work of Poggio Bracciolini, who was a copier of manuscripts. Sometime around 1400, Poggio developed the "humanistic" script, which was, in fact, based on twelfth century script and attempted to revive the writing of the Romans. Poggio toured the monastaries of Europe and came up with a copy of Vitruvius which he rescued from the "filth and dirt" in which he found it, and brought the manuscript to Florence, which was the center of humanism and the home of the "rebirth" of the arts.

Here, the giants of the Renaissance thought they were creating a "new" architecture. Here Donatello, the sculptor, was beginning to sculpt "statues that began to look like living men," such as his famous statue of St. George—the embodiment of Vitruvius' theory of eurythmy. Filippo Brunelleschi, one of the first of the great early Renaissance men, put the words of Vitruvius into physical architectural form. Brunelleschi was a perfect disciple of Vitruvius, being a "universal" craftsman, since he was a goldsmith, sculptor, painter, engineer and architect all in one. Brunelleschi's churches exemplified the Vitruvian concept of space, and Brunelleschi ventured further into perspective and dimension.

One of Filippo Brunelleschi's contemporaries said that he made the current style of architecture "speak Latin"; in other words, his work assumed a classical form. For example, he revived the circular plan used in Vitruvius' suggestions for Augustan classical temples and carried over into early Christian times, as in his own unfinished *S. Maria degli Angeli*. He revived classical proportions in the colonnades and pediments of the *Ospedale degli Innocenti*. Brunelleschi has been justly called the "most creative scientist" of his age as well as one of its greatest artists. His scientific achievements include not only the study of perspective but his construction of the dome of the Cathedral of Florence, which was thought impossible to build by his fellow artists—and the source of both achievements are in the writings of Vitruvius.

All of the masters of the early Renaissance show the influence of the writing of Vitruvius, including Michelangelo, Raphael, and his fellow Bramante. It is said that Raphael hired a scholar to render a private translation of Vitruvius' ten books.

And the Baths of Caracalla, drawn by Palladio, one of the truly gifted architects of the early Renaissance, might have come from the drawing board of Vitruvius himself. Palladio's townhouses and country villas in and around Venetia, particularly around Vicenza and along the Brenta, show his creative utilization of Vitruvius' studies of Ancient Greek buildings and execute to the finest detail the admonitions of Vitruvius for proper design for a residence. The influence of Palladio extended throughout Europe and is especially evident in England in the architecture of Sir Christopher Wren.

All of these men of genius were deeply indebted to Vitruvius and applied the rules and purposes of Vitruvius to their works. But, as the mark of the Renaissance, they carried their efforts beyond simply duplicating building forms of antiquity, and reached for the magnificent creative heights marked by the flourishing Renaissance period.

It is interesting to note that as each new movement of art and architecture flourishes, a certain snobbery mushrooms, and at the height of the Renaissance knowledge of Vitruvius was indicative of a certain class superiority. Appreciation of Greek art and architecture was the "taste" of the day, and certain writers concerned themselves only with Vitruvius' *Orders* and tended to regard the Romanesque and Gothic periods of Roman architecture as "barbaric" and intolerable.

Following the decline of the Renaissance and the flowing form and space of the Baroque period, we see again the principles of Vitruvius being discarded with the advent of the Rococo style where the senseless superfluity of applied decorations to buildings began to dissolve the purity of the earlier Renaissance work.

It is not until the Industrial Revolution with the development of iron and steel that we see again a massive release of imaginative energies in the direction of another "new" art and architecture, utilizing the new materials and the new technology at hand. And once again the pages of Vitruvius are consulted.

Architects of the Bauhaus founded in Dessau, Germany, in 1925 in the highly academic stylistic classical orders, openly rebelled at the very thought of using new materials such as steel and glass and new mass production methods. Then, unconsciously in their revolt, they returned to the fundamental truths of Vitruvius, and his principles were soon to be evidenced again in a form of architecture which was at first shocking, but as the artistic concept of the use of new materials available became more and more evident, this "new" architecture moved forward in its universal scope.

Again the Vitruvian truth that not invention but the use made by invention is the architect's measure of genius was self-evident. Steel set the modern architect free to design buildings in every shape his creative mind could conceive, and the very movement of civilization which produced the Machine Age produced a radical change in the living habits of modern man. The old materials—brick, stone, and wood—had bound earlier buildings to the confines of simple geometric designs, conventional and strict forms set (even the masterpieces) solidly upon the earth. New materials released the architect from earlier constrictions and limitations.

As Vasparas saw in Donatello's sculpture a man who looked like men, living men, so did modern man looking at David Hare's sculpture of man made of steel and wire see an image of himself. The difference lies in that one man lived in a world of Carrara marble, the second in a world of steel. But both pieces were honest and apropos of the time of their creation.

Walter Gropius, one of the founders of Bauhaus, has said: "A breach has been made with the past, which allows us to envisage a new aspect of architecture corresponding to the technical civilization of the age we live in; the morphology of dead styles has been destroyed and we are returning to honesty of thought and feelings. The general public, formerly profoundly indifferent to everything to do with building, has been shaken out of its torpor; personal interest in architecture as something that concerns every one of us in our daily lives has been widely aroused and the broad lines of its future development are clearly discernible." It was Vitruvius who wrote: "If designs for private houses are to be correct, we must take note at the outset of the countries in which they are built . . . the materials available, the needs of the occupant."

The Bauhaus was devoted to training artists in a principled creative manner and the combining of manual skills with scholarship. These workshops were really laboratories for working out practical new designs not only for housing, industry, and government, but for present-day utilitarian articles and improving the original models for mass production. Yet the founders were fully conscious that if mechanization became an end unto itself, it would be an unmitigated calamity, robbing life of half its fullness and variety by stunting men and women into sub-human robot-like automatons.

They knew it was essential for civilization to protect the delicate works of craftsmen such as Cellini and Faberge, as well as to encourage and develop the talents of such modern craftsmen as Otto Berger and Marcel Breuer, who were designing equally beautiful objects for daily use which could be mass produced and universally owned and enjoyed. Gropius writes, "Whether a design be the outcome of knack or creative impulse depends on individual propensity. But if what we call art cannot be taught or learnt, a thorough knowledge of principles and sureness of hand can be. Both are as necessary for the artist of genius as for the artisan."

Compare this with Vitruvius' statement almost twenty centuries earlier: "It follows, therefore, that architects who have aimed at acquiring manual skill without scholarship have never been able to reach a position of authority to correspond to their pains, while those who relied on theory and scholarship were obviously hunting the shadow, not the substance. But those who have a thorough knowledge of both, like men armed at all points, have sooner obtained their object and carried authority with them."

In the beginning of any phase of "new" architecture, the artist begins with the private dwellings of individuals. This explanation lies quite simply in the fact that the owner of a house is less restricted by commerce, or by the traditions of institutions. In a private dwelling the architect and the owner have created their own marriage, where the architect, conscious of the social position, philosophy, and financial limitations of the owner, synthesizes everything into a harmonious creation. So long as man is living, architecture will be a living and flowing form of art, expressing the man and the age.

The atrium styled house of Augustus on Palatine Hill was, according to Suetonius in his biography of Augustus, "neither particularly big, nor strikingly decorated. It had only short colonnades of peperin, a volcanic rock, and its rooms contained neither marble nor mosaic floors." This was the house of the man who longed to restore Rome to the customs and austerity of his forefathers. The mausoleum he erected to contain the ashes of the Julian family was not ornate like the imitative Greek ones which offended Vitrivius, but reminiscent of the tombs found on the roads leading to Rome, the tombs of the men who had died to establish the Republic.

Naturally, with such a man Vitruvius had immediate rapport. For Augustus, Vitruvius explained that as man began to assemble and indulge in social intercourse, he devised shelter from the wild elements and fierce animals. This man constructed his dwellings "out of the materials on hand," some building them "of green boughs, some dug caves on the mountainsides, others in imitation of the swallow building a nest made places of refuge out of mud and twigs."

AN ARCHITECT FOR ALL AGES

In the geographical replacements of man Vitruvius observes for architects that concern should be taken in selecting the sites for cities in locales that are desirable for the erection of buildings, and urges that the private dwellings be made out of materials indigenous to the site, easily available and practical for use.

"As for the kind of materials used, this does not depend upon the architect for the reason that all kinds of materials are not found in all places alike. Consequently the question of approving any work may be considered under three heads; that is, delicacy of workmanship, sumptuousness, and design. When it appears that a work has been carried out sumptuously, the owner will be praised for the great outlay he has authorized; when delicately, the master workman will be approved for his execution; but when symmetry and proportion lend it an imposing effect, then the glory of it will belong to the architect."

As Vitruvius explains, houses are built to suit different classes of persons, but in all houses, large or small or for rich or poor, there should be private rooms such as bedrooms, bathrooms, and rooms used for personal purposes. These rooms should be areas into which nobody has the right to enter without invitation. The common spaces are those which anyone is free to enter, such as entrance courts or any outdoor areas used for group encounters, and should be consistent with the freedom for the essential social intercourse they represent.

Years later, Frank Lloyd Wright, discussing in his autobiography the building of a house, the now famous Winslow house, wrote: "My sense of 'wall' was no longer the side of the box. It was enclosure of space affording protection against storm or heat only when needed. But it is also to bring the outside world into the house and let the inside go outside. In this sense, I was working away at a wall, and bringing it towards the function of a screen, a means of opening up a space which, as control of building materials improved, would finally permit the free use of the whole space without affecting the soundness of the structure.

"The climate being what it was, violent in extremes of heat and cold, damp and dry, dark and bright, I gave a broad protecting roof shelter to the whole, getting back into the purpose for which the cornice was originally designed. At this time, I saw a house primarily as a livable space under ample shelter. I liked the sense of shelter in the look of the building. I still like it. The house began to associate with the ground and become natural to the prairie site." And he adds, "Human use and comfort should have intimate possession of every interior . . . should be felt in every exterior."

Of all the arts, public opinion controls architecture more than any other form, for society employs those architects who conform to its demands and needs. An architect's right to expound his personal theories is limited to the passivity or congeniality of his client. But for an architect to create an architecture, he must find public acceptance. The architecture which has survived (like the theories of Vitruvius) is that which people have taken to themselves, recognizing it as their own and expressive of the true organic nature of mankind.

Individual houses of great architects are not merely dwellings but essays in organic materials, regardless of their aesthetic mastery or their virtuosity in structure. As Corbusier said: "Human creations that survive are those that produce emotions, not merely those that are useful." And Vitruvius wrote, "The architect should be equipped with knowledge of many branches of study and varied kinds of learning, for it is by his judgment that all works done by the other arts are put to test. He should be both naturally gifted and amenable to instruction."

As such, the architect of today is cognizant (as was Vitruvius in the plans he devised for towns in the

AN ARCHITECT FOR ALL AGES

Roman Empire) that the ultimate glory of architecture and the ultimate triumph of architecture lie in city planning. With the ever increasing problems of population explosion, urban clutter, and the lack of social and physical communication, city planning must encompass the brains and activities of specialists in many fields. The shortsighted vision of the real-estate developer of the nineteenth and twentieth centuries has produced the inadequate, anachronistic, and, in many instances, obsolete cities that we know today. With the increased usage of automobile transportation, new road systems, ever changing building techniques, landscaped open spaces, architecture must satisfy modern man's needs both practically and aesthetically and relate to the areas in which he lives and works.

In Brazil Oscar Niemeyer and other architects collaborating with master planner Lucio Costag built an urban center, Brazilia, that is one great architectural pattern of spaces, forms, lights, shadows, colors, textures, landscapes, and dwellings, all a setting for the movable pawn on this contemporary chessboard—modern man living and working in a space-orientated age of atomic energy. While not addressing itself to the great socio-economic problems which face that nation's people, nonetheless it is an outstanding planning accomplishment for South American man. So, too, Corbusier's plan for Chandigarh has brought a new city to the man of India.

These two new cities are areas widely spaced on our globe in which the architectural forms co-exist with nature. Since modern man lives in a mechanized age, the factories in which he spends a great part of his time must be light, transparent, conducive to work, both for psychological and sociological effects. The home to which he returns must coordinate outdoor and indoor living with the introduction of true works of art as objects for use in his everyday existence.

AN ARCHITECT FOR ALL AGES

With walls of glass, mighty cantilevers, interlacing spirals, floating walls, and penetrating cubes of air, all children of steel and reinforced concrete, the modern architect can help create a modern city for the modern man, a city to inspire civic pride such as was evidenced in Greece in the days of Pericles, in Rome in the days of Augustus, in Europe in the Renaissance. We have only to heed the advice of the architect, Vitruvius, whose wisdom spanned centuries when he urged the use of materials and skills available and properly adapted to the needs and environment of man.

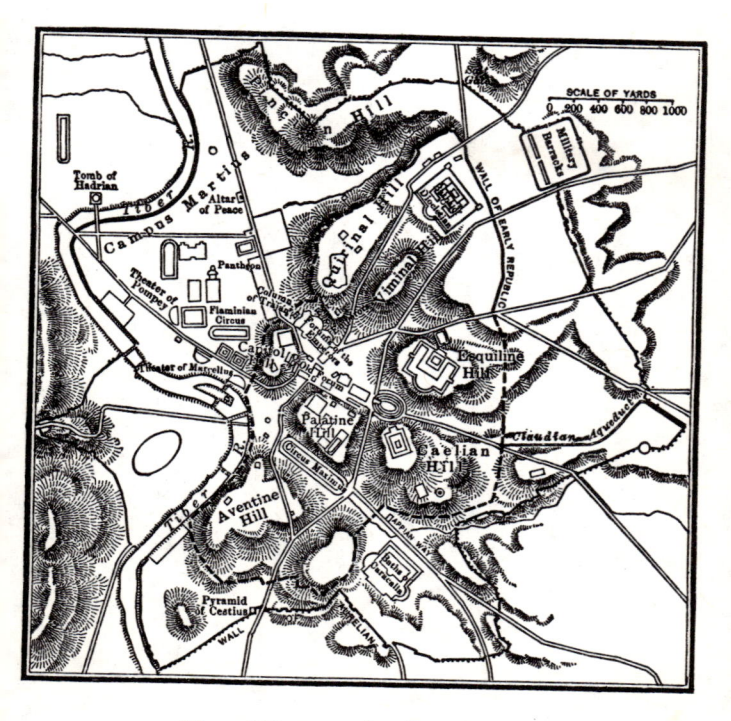

Map of Rome under the Emperors

Pontius Pilate delivering Christ to the mob

PONTIUS PILATE: THE JUDGE WHO CHANGED HISTORY

By Paul L. Maier

*D*uring the smoldering Mediterranean summer of 1961, a group of Italian archaeologists were carefully excavating an ancient theater at Caesarea in Palestine. The "dig" was making slow progress, uncovering items of interest for scholarly journals but nothing important enough for the wire services. Then one of the workers dislodged a two-by-three foot stone beneath a flight of steps in the ancient structure and painstakingly removed the debris of two thousand years still encrusting it. Only then did he notice that the bottom side, which had been buried, bore some kind of inscription. Clearly, the stone had been used earlier for another purpose. He summoned the leader of the expedition.

Antonio Frova, guiding the Caesarea dig, cleaned out the lettering with a brush and tried to make sense of the inscription. Suddenly his eyes widened in disbelief, while his face was cut by a vast grin. He shouted for his colleagues to come over and share the moment of triumph. Eyes squinted, smiles blazed, and the Italian archaeological expedition exploded into a cacophony of cheers. The left third of the inscription had been chipped away, but Frova reconstructed it in short order. The following Latin had been cut into the stone in three-inch lettering:

<blockquote>
CAESARIENS. TIBERIEVM
PONTIVS PILATVS
PRAEFECTVS IVDAEAE
DEDIT
</blockquote>

"Pontius Pilatus, Prefect of Judea, has presented the Tiberiéum to the Caesareans." This simple but proud sentence marked the first inscriptional evidence for the existence of Pontius Pilate ever to be discovered, the kind of literally *tangible* information which is still missing for such other greats in history as Homer or Herodotus, Socrates or Jesus.

This discovery added dramatically to our knowledge about one of the most fascinating yet enigmatic figures of the past. His name is repeated every moment at Masses being conducted across the world, and each Sunday by eight hundred million Christians as they recite the words of the Creed. In that sense, he is easily the most famous Roman of them all, for many who know little about a Caesar or Augustus or even Nero still confess the words, "I believe in Jesus Christ . . . who . . . suffered under Pontius Pilate."

And now Frova had discovered the name of history's most familiar judge in stone. A century ago, such a find would have dealt a mortal blow to the radical critics—one of them the German scholar Bruno Bauer—who denied that Jesus or Pilate ever lived. But since almost no one shares such extreme views today, Frova's find was important for other reasons.

For one thing it was strange that Pilate used Latin for his official inscription rather than Greek, the common language of the eastern Mediterranean. He probably did so in tribute to Tiberius, the Roman emperor who had sent him to govern Judea and for whom Pilate named his building. (Whether the Tiberiéum was a temple or civic structure is still under investigation by scholars.)

But more important is the fact that Pilate is called "Prefect of Judea" in this inscription. Pick up any reference work on the Bible or any encyclopedia, look for the entry "Pontius Pilate," and you will invariably find the man called a "procurator," a mistaken term based on what has now proven to be anachronisms used by the first historians who refer to Pilate. While both titles can be translated as governor, the Roman prefect had more military responsibilities than the procurator. But how difficult it is to change traditional history; Frova published his findings in 1961, and yet the 1968 edition of the *Encyclopaedia Britannica* still calls Pilate a procurator, as do other reference sets.

Hardly due to any personal achievement, Pontius Pilate became a pin in one of the hinges of destiny simply because he happened to preside at a trial which became the central event in history. But for his judgment on the day called Good Friday, a faith shared by nearly a billion people today might not have been born. At least it would not have developed as we know it. It is idle to speculate what might have happened had Pilate quashed the case of Jesus of Nazareth, for with the word *Staurotheto* ("Let him be crucified") Pilate condemned Jesus, Christianity was born, that particular Friday became "Good," and the judge would never be forgotten.

If Pilate's is one of the most remembered names in

history, it is also one of the least popular. Though the early Christian church intended the wording of the Creed ("Suffered under Pontius Pilate") merely to document the event, not necessarily to assign guilt, the blame developed anyway and, for the last seventeen centuries, Pilate has had an unusually bad press.

The most terrifying — and certainly imaginative — punishments were invented for him: torture, insanity, exile, compulsive hand-washing, suicide, drowning, decapitation, being swallowed by the earth, and even that ancient punishment for parricide: being sewn up in an ox-hide with a cock, a viper, and a monkey, and pitched into a river. Medieval legends would add the familiar stories of his restless corpse, accompanied by squadrons of demons, disrupting localities from France to Switzerland, causing storms, earthquakes, and other havoc.

On the basis of the earliest sources, however, it is clear that nothing of the sort ever happened to Pilate, let alone his corpse. Much later, Lenten preaching to the contrary, one of the earliest church fathers, Tertullian, claimed that Pilate "was a Christian in his conscience." Greek Orthodoxy canonized his wife. To this day, October 27 is St. Procla's Day in their calendar, while the Ethiopian church even recognizes the 25th of June as "St. Pilate and St. Procla's Day."

Sinner or saint, Pilate quickly became one of the most controversial figures in history. But what about the true Pontius Pilate, the man behind the legend? Is anything more known about the famously infamous judge today?

Frova's discovery of the Pilate inscription was a first step. And a very careful rereading of the historical sources also provides several new facts as well as a host of clues toward a more accurate portrait of Pontius Pilate.

We now have more evidence on his background and

ancestry. His name alone provides two valuable hints. "Pontius," the family name, can be identified as a prominent clan name among the Samnites, hill cousins of the Latin Romans who lived along the Apennine mountain spine southeast of Rome. A scrappy breed, the Samnites had almost conquered Rome in several fierce wars. The Pontii were of noble blood, but when Rome finally absorbed the Samnites, their aristocracy was demoted to the Roman equestrian order, which was second only to the senatorial or patrician class at Rome. The name still lives on in Italy, the most famous representative of the family today being motion-picture producer Carlo Ponti, husband of Sophia Loren.

But it is Pilate's second name "Pilatus" which proves almost conclusively that he was indeed of Samnite origin. Pilatus means "Armed-with-a-Javelin." The *pilum* or javelin was a balanced missile six feet long, half wooden handle and half pointed iron shaft, which Samnite mountaineers hurled at their enemies with devastating effect. The Romans quickly copied the weapon, and it was the *pilum,* in fact, which had made the Roman Empire possible.

Pilate ruled as Prefect of Judea from 26 to 36 A.D., the second longest tenure of any first-century Roman governor in Palestine. The very length of his office contradicts the usual impression of Pilate as an incompetent official, for it is doubtful that the Roman emperor Tiberius, who insisted on good provincial administration, would have retained Pilate in office so long had he been the political cripple of popular repute. Nor was the prefecture of Judea a petty post staffed by dissatisfied officials, an impression almost universal among Biblical novelists: in that case, Pilate might easily have resigned his post for greener pastures elsewhere in the Roman Empire.

He did, however, find the governorship of Judea a most taxing experience, and several vignettes of Pilate show the remarkably "modern" problems an ancient administrator had to face. Aside from his familiar role on Good Friday, there are five separate incidents involving Pilate which are reported by other ancient historians, notably Josephus and Philo. Because it seems that Pilate blundered in each of these instances, he has been roundly faulted for his performance as governor in most histories since that time. And yet a close study of these episodes would suggest that Pilate, while hardly a master of diplomacy, was at least trying to make the best of very difficult administrative situations.

In what came to be called "the affair of the Roman standards," Pilate's troops once marched into Jerusalem carrying medallions with the emperor's image or bust among their regimental standards. This action provoked a five-day mass demonstration by Jews at the provincial capital, Caesarea, which protested the effigies as a violation of Jewish law concerning engraved images (Exodus 20:4-5). Pilate finally relented and ordered the offensive standards removed.

Later in his administration, he built an aqueduct to improve Jerusalem's water supply, but paid for it with funds from the Temple treasury. This sparked another riot, which was put down only after bloodshed, even though Pilate had cautioned his troops not to use swords.

While this seems a grotesque example of malfeasance, a case could be made that Jewish sacred writings permitted expenditure of surplus Temple funds for such civic needs as water supply, and it would seem that Pilate must have had some cooperation from priestly authorities in Jerusalem. He could not simply have plundered the sacrosanct Temple treasury: gentiles were forbidden on pain of death to enter the Temple interior, where the sacred treasure was stored. Any such violation would have led to Pilate's recall. And since the aqueduct fed cisterns below the Temple, building operations could hardly have been undertaken in that area without at least tacit approval of the religious authorities. Apparently, the subsequent outcry was a protest of the people, not the authorities, who may even have warned Pilate in advance of the approaching demonstrations in Jerusalem.

On another occasion, Pilate set up several golden shields in his Jerusalem headquarters, which, unlike the standards, bore no images whatever, only a bare inscription of dedication to Tiberius. And yet the people protested even the imageless shields, but this time Pilate refused to remove them. He could, and perhaps did, point to the precedent of Jews in Alexandria who adorned the very walls of their synagogues with gilded shields in honor of the Roman emperor. But Alexandria was not Jerusalem, and the Judeans protested to Tiberius, who ordered Pilate to transfer the shields to a temple in Caesarea.

Not long after this bizarre affair, Pilate made his entry on the stage of history as judge of Jesus of Nazareth. Since his role here is so very familiar, only the new insights into this most dramatic of trials need be presented. However critically the New Testament may be interpreted, it seems clear that Pilate was convinced of Jesus' innocence and tried several means to dispose of his case without passing sentence: change of venue —transferring the case to the neighboring governor, Herod Antipas; Passover amnesty—the alternative of Jesus or Bar-abbas; crowd psychology—trying to win sympathy for the accused; and quashing the case for lack of evidence—"I have found him not guilty of any of the charges." Even the final hand-washing was symbolic.

The turning point in the trial, however, came near its close when the prosecution made its famous statement: "If you let this man go free, you are not Caesar's friend; for every one who makes himself a king sets himself against Caesar." It was after this challenge that Pilate decided, however reluctantly, to sentence Jesus to the cross. What changed his mind at *this* particular point?

Good Friday, as can be shown from the sources, most probably fell a year after the episode of the golden shields. Tiberius' letter, which had ordered Pilate to remove those shields, also warned him to uphold all the religious and political customs of his Judean subjects. Now, if the people of Jerusalem protested to the emperor over something so comparatively small as several imageless shields, how much more serious would be their protest, again over Pilate's head, in a case which they obviously considered of much greater religious importance.

Even the detail that Pilate would not be "Caesar's friend" if he released Jesus is highly significant. To be Caesar's friend (*Amicus Caesaris*) was a special rank in Rome. A person so honored could wear a golden ring with the emperor's image and move in an elite fraternity open only to Romans high in governmental service. But loss of this status usually involved disgrace, exile, or even suicide.

The prosecution, then, warned Pilate that he would be condoning treason if he failed to punish someone who seditiously claimed kingship. They need not have reminded Pilate that he would also be disobeying the emperor in failing to uphold local religious law concerning blasphemy, for Jesus claimed to be the "Son of God." For Pilate, such a double indictment would have meant anything from loss of office to compulsory suicide. The trial was over—also for the judge.

This raises, of course, the extremely sensitive question of responsibility for the crucifixion of Jesus of Nazareth. An amazing amount of bad thinking has gone into answering this vexed query, with very tragic con-

PONTIUS PILATE: THE JUDGE WHO CHANGED HISTORY

sequences. There can be no doubt that Pontius Pilate had the final responsibility for announcing the verdict and executing sentence. The role of the Judean prosecution, however, has been vigorously debated, and even denied entirely.

The priestly establishment in Jerusalem was, however, involved in the prosecution. This can be demonstrated also outside the New Testament from purely Jewish sources and traditions as, for example, in *Sanhedrin* 43a of The Babylonian Talmud. But to follow Medieval Christianity in developing an anti-Semitic attitude from Jewish involvement in the trial of Jesus would be utterly illogical and irresponsible. The prosecution was acting in absolute good faith—Jesus, in their view, had committed supreme blasphemy and was a potential seditionist — but that prosecution was not even representative of the Jewish people of that time. Indeed, the Talmud vigorously condemns Annas and Caiaphas, the leaders of the priestly establishment. Finally, to be anti-Semitic because of Good Friday would be as ridiculous as to hate Italians because a few of their forebears once threw Christians to the lions!

Strangely, it was no imbroglio with his Jewish subjects which caused Pilate's recall but rather a furor involving Samaritans, those half-breed cousins of the Jews who lived in mid-Palestine. An obscure pseudo-prophet with Messianic ambitions promised the Samaritans he would uncover some sacred temple utensils which Moses had supposedly buried on their sacred Mt. Gerizim, and a host of credulous Samaritans gathered to witness the spectacle.

Because the multitude had come armed with weapons — perhaps also to prevent the people from being exploited—Pilate ordered his troops to block the route of ascent. It came to a pitched battle. Pilate's forces won, and the leaders of the uprising were executed.

Here again, Pilate's action, while certainly harsh, was no more than what other Roman governors had done under similar circumstances to subdue what had developed into an armed sedition astride the main artery of Palestine.

The Samaritan Senate, however, complained to Pilate's superior, the proconsul of Syria, who ordered Pilate to return to Rome to answer the charges against him. Pilate had no choice in the matter, and departed for Rome late in 36 A.D.

Was Judge Pontius Pilate himself judged in Rome? Perhaps we shall never know. The historical record of Josephus, the principal source, breaks off with this intriguing sentence: "But before he reached Rome, Tiberius had already died." Tiberius' successor, the emperor Gaius Caligula, either heard Pilate's case or, more probably, quashed it, as he did most of the cases carried over from Tiberius' administration.

The traditional view of Pilate's fate is extremely negative, as indicated, and the various Pilate legends became exercises in morbid imagination. However, the tradition of Pilate's suicide is very strong indeed because it dates back to the fourth-century church historian Eusebius. Yet there are difficulties in Eusebius' evidence, and the more important testimony of the earlier church father Origen plus conclusions from first-century historians decidedly contradict the suicide story. Nothing grossly negative, it seems, ever befell Pilate.

In all probability, the fate of the ex-Prefect of Judea lay more in the direction of a retired government official, a pensioned Roman magistrate emeritus, than in anything more disastrous. Possibly he was a man just as satisfied that history did not record his last years. He may even have spent his time looking for an answer to the question he once asked, under circumstances he may well have forgotten: "What is truth?"

The Pilate stone, uncovered by Italian archaeologist Antonio Frova in the summer of 1961. Translation of the inscription reads: Pontius Pilate, Prefect of Judea, has presented the Tiberieum to the Caesareans.

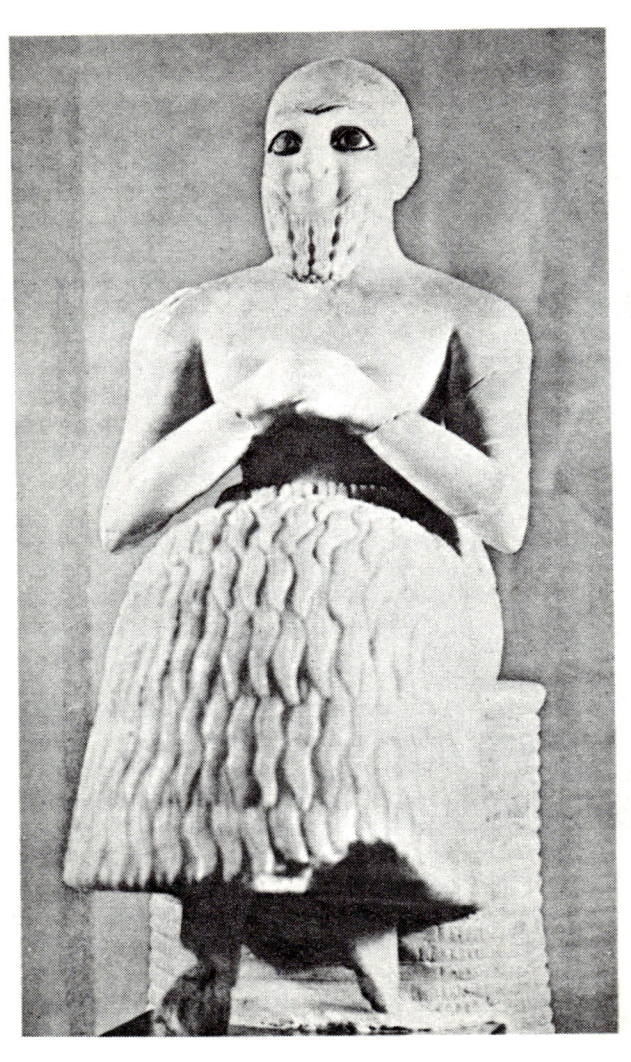

The Priest Abihil of the Temple of Ishtar at Mari (Sumer). Circa 2900-2685 (?) B.C.

THE KEY TO THE ANCIENT MEDITERRANEAN: SYRIA, LEBANON AND ISRAEL

By Michael Grant

*T*he key to the ancient history of the Mediterranean, and to a great deal of its modern history as well, is the easternmost of all its shores—the region extending between the peninsula of Asia Minor on the north and the valley and delta of the Nile on the south.

Those two countries which it spans and joins are well defined and labeled. The one, with its hinterland, is Asiatic Turkey (Anatolia) and the other is Egypt. But the vital area in between has no single name or identity. From top to bottom on the map, it nowadays comprises the Hatay (an appendage of Turkey), most of Syria, Lebanon, and Israel in its current enlarged form. The whole region was known comprehensively to the ancients as Syria and was described more recently by Arab Nationalists as Greater Syria—and sometimes it is vaguely known as the Levant, though that designation normally covers the shores of Anatolia as well.

Yet, for all this ambiguity, the region preeminently deserves study in its own right, as a single unit. And this it has very rarely received—partly because large portions of the territory have usually been inaccessible to travelers, and partly also because students of the Mediterranean, other than Biblical specialists, have generally been motivated by a conscious or unconscious pro-Western prejudice which has caused them to underestimate the significance of the most easterly coasts of that sea.

To the ancients the land seemed destined for prosperity by nature. In spite of the southern latitude and the dangers of unpredictable drought, there were rainfalls in late autumn and early spring, and the plains beside and between the mountains were fertile. "Figs there were in it, and grapes," said an Egyptian visitor. "It had more wine than water. Its trees bore every fruit. Barley was there and wheat. There was no limit to the kinds of cattle. Plentiful was its honey, abundant its olives."

And yet Syria and Lebanon and Israel, so greatly blessed by nature, were also visited with a special curse. On the map, this area looks clearly definable by Turkey, Egypt, the Mediterranean, and—to the east —the desert. But the long Mediterranean coastline is vulnerable, and the eastern approaches to the region show that its apparent definition and unity is an illusion. It did not need three modern Israeli-Arab wars to point out the territory is, in fact, grievously lacking in the natural unity which enabled other Mediterranean countries such as Italy, Greece, Egypt, or Spain to grow at different times into defensible national states.

The whole large area of Syria-Lebanon-Israel contains a series of uplifted limestone ridges which, instead of forming its boundaries, run straight through it parallel to the coast. At the northern extremity there are Mounts Amanus and Casius, followed by Bargylus (Jebel Ansariya), and next comes the Lebanon range which is the most imposing of the coastal massifs. South of Lebanon are the Galilee hills, and after them Mount Carmel, the northern-most point of the Samaritan plateau, succeeded by the Judaean plateau which stretches down as far as Sinai.

The lowlands beside and between these folds are long funnels open to every sort of influence and invasion from the north and south by external peoples covetous of all this wealth and fertility. The two principal tubular areas inviting such encroachments are the coastal regions and then—beyond the first ranges and parallel to them, from 20 to 60 miles distant from the sea—a continuous depression running through the valleys of the Orontes, Litani (Leontes), and Jordan and on through the Dead Sea, deepest of all subsidences in the earth's crust, to the Gulf of Eilat or Akaba.

But it is not only through the extremities of these funnels that the coastland is vulnerable, for the mountains are also broken by passes that have eternally served as passages for acquisitive armies. And behind the openings, through further uplands and deserts, stretch back the classic routes into the sources of the aggressions—and civilizations—which it was the destiny of these lands to receive and absorb.

Accordingly this area never became a single national state but remained a conglomeration of small units. This was also true of Greece, and yet it achieved greatness. But Greece, except for occasional dramatic events, was left alone for centuries to work out its destiny. The small states of Syria, Lebanon, and Israel, on the other hand, were almost never free of invasions by the giants of Asia and Egypt—and so the territory, for all its resources, remained in turmoil, an amorphous political and cultural quicksand.

THE ANCIENT MEDITERRANEAN

"To me," said Paul Morand, "the Mediterranean is a pit surrounded by tiers of seats over which the nations are leaning, all crowded together. The same piece has been played for thousands of years." In Syria and Lebanon and Israel the scenery of this theatre was built of elements that were peculiarly inflammable—also peculiarly creative, since out of the conflagrations came a mixture which exercised a gigantic influence upon developments throughout the Mediterranean world.

The movement of external and alien peoples into this region began at an exceedingly early date. Men and women living in caves on Mount Carmel in the tenth millennium B.C., who made use of reaping knives or sickles, may well have come from the more northerly foothill (Tauros-Zagros) area where decisive developments were made possible by the presence of wheat, barley, sheep, and goats—all vital aids to civilization—in their wild and natural forms which gradually gave way to domesticated varieties.

Then, before 6000 B.C., a comparatively advanced culture developed in the extreme northwestern corner of Syria. Here, on the lower Orontes, the various advances in agriculture and stock-breeding registered during the previous millennia were concentrated in the nearly 400 square miles of the Amik plain, which was close to the great westward curve of the Euphrates and therefore accessible to movements of population and culture from the east.

However, it was not by the land route from the east but by the sea route from the west and south that the most decisive early influences came to bear upon the region. This was because of Egypt, which gradually achieved a national unity wholly beyond the capacity of the Syria-Lebanon-Israel area. This unity was made possible, indeed necessary, by the Nile—which simply had to be controlled and irrigated in a coordinated fashion if the people on its shores were to survive. The

Sumerians in southern Mesopotamia had been presented with a similar problem by the erratic Tigris and Euphrates, and had partially solved it by an efficient city-state organization. Egypt went much further, in two stages.

First, two kingdoms were established—Lower Egypt, which was the Nile delta, and Upper Egypt, which lay south of it and stretched down towards the Sudan. Then, by the initiative of the latter they were united (around 3200 B.C.), becoming immeasurably the strongest state which the region, and probably the world, had seen thus far. Yet although they learned how to navigate the Nile, it remained, apparently, for the people of the Syrian coast to teach them how to build effective seagoing ships. Egypt was exceedingly interested in this coast because its own homeland was very short of timber, the local woods not being very serviceable for building ships. The Egyptians were therefore eager to obtain the fir, cedar, pine, cypress, and juniper with which northern Syria and Lebanon were once rich—though nowadays erosion and human devastation have long since stripped their slopes.

The town which provided the necessary harbor and expertise was Byblos, on the coast of what was later called Phoenicia beneath the Lebanon range. Byblos stood at the northernmost point of Egypt's normal sphere of influence and virtually possessed a monopoly of trade with that country. Indeed, during the third millennium B.C. this city of rectangular houses and cobbled streets even had an Egyptian temple, measuring over 80 and later over 90 feet long. The construction of a shrine of this considerable size suggests the presence of a substantial commercial colony from Egypt. Byblos acted as a distribution center for Egyptian exports of papyrus, for which indeed "byblos" (Bible) became the standard name. The city also exported copper and other metals brought in by caravan from the north.

The people of the Lebanese and Syrian coastal lands were experts at every kind of woodwork, and it was probably they who both constructed and to a large extent manned the first Egyptian seagoing ships, thus becoming the first professional Mediterranean shipbuilders and sailors. "The seaman," said Joseph Conrad, "looks upon the Mediterranean as a man may look at a vast nursery in an old, old mansion, where innumerable generations of his own people have learned to walk. It has led mankind gently from headland to headland, from bay to bay, from island to island, out into the promise of worldwide oceans." And the earliest initiatives seem to have been taken by these sailors from Byblos who created and navigated the seagoing vessels seen on Egyptian monuments.

Byblos, and the coast extending to the south of it, was colonized by peoples speaking a north Semitic dialect. They had already arrived by 2500 B.C.—and perhaps a good deal earlier since Lebanese and Syrian mountains and rivers mostly possessed names of early Semitic origin. Peoples speaking this sort of language, already profoundly mixed in race, had long been prominent in Mesopotamia; but a tradition, which may be right, held that these arrivals on the Levantine shores had come overland not from the east but from more primitive territories in western Arabia.

Copper statuettes of the period indicate that they were a herdsman type, familiar over large areas of the Near East—short, stocky people with pronounced chins, trim beards and swept-back plaited hair, clothed in short kilts and broad belts fastened with tasseled cords. They called their new homeland Canaan, a name which later came to be used for territories extending over a much wider area.

But they were not to remain undisturbed, since Syria was deeply vulnerable to the great wanderings of many peoples who devastated Mesopotamia and the rest of the Middle East towards the end of the third millennium B.C. In *circa* 2100 the Egyptian temple at Byblos was burned down, and the city's life and culture changed abruptly. Perhaps this event was part of the convulsions which at about this time inundated Syria with a further wave of Semitic invaders.

These newcomers, the Amorites, were induced by the advanced prosperity of the land they now occupied to adopt some of its culture and to form highly developed though small and inevitably precarious city-states. These included Aleppo between the Orontes mouth and the Euphrates, Carchemish on the present Turco-Syrian frontier, Qatna (Mishrife) behind the Lebanon range, and the commercial center of Mari (Tell Hariri) on the Euphrates near the border of Syria and Iraq.

The 20,000 surviving documents of Mari's archives, written in old Babylonian cuneiform (wedge-shaped) characters, display in startling detail how complex the international position in this part of the world had already become. Dating from the 18th century B.C. onwards, they mention more than 30 separate states linked or divided, in modern style, by the diplomatic interactions of intrigue, commercial and cultural exchanges, and warfare. The civilization of this area was a blend of many influences, and certain architectural and artistic features were imitated by the far-off Cretans whose own distinctive civilization was now reaching its zenith.

One Amorite was Shamsi-Adad I (*circa* 1814-1782) who ruled over the Assyrians (distant relatives of his own people), and created a powerful state in the undulating, well-watered pasture lands of the upper Tigris. The Assyrians were masters of a formidable blend of first-class archery, administrative ability, and cold-blooded diplomacy; and they drew much of their power from outposts in Asia Minor which provided them with copper. Mixed with tin, this made the bronze that gave them better weapons and agricultural tools than had been known before.

When, therefore, Shamsi-Adad set up his own son at Mari and established close relationships with Qatna, Aleppo, and Carchemish, and above all when he set up a boastful monument on the Lebanon coast, a conflict with the other great power, Egypt, was inevitable. For the monument was in an area which was normally within the sphere of the Egyptians, who had been using Byblos as a center of expansion. Their exports reached Qatna and they exercised some sort of control, perhaps economic more than political, over most of the Lebanon coast and Bekaa plain.

Assyria, as it turned out, was unable to compete with Egypt at this junction since it was eclipsed by Babylonia—which was too remote to be active so far west. But, instead, a perilous new threat now came upon Egypt and its Syrian dependencies from the mountainous territories north of Mesopotamia. From these regions a people of uncertain linguistic affinities, the Hurrians, extended their influence and power over huge areas, which they kept under control by the mounted warriors and chariots that were their specialty. Although these people possessed little art of their own (except a fine type of pottery), they absorbed the Mesopotamian and other cultures which they brought into the areas they infiltrated.

By the 16th century the Hurrians had established the powerful kingdom of Mitanni in northwestern Mesopotamia, and thus directly or indirectly controlled most of Syria. Perhaps there was even an outpost as far south as Gaza, where excavations have disclosed burials of men with their horses which suggest the influence of Mitanni. But the kingdom's principal capital on the Syrian shore was at the other extremity of the coastline—at Alalakh (Tell Atchana) near the mouth of the Orontes. In this terminal region of trade routes to the Mediterranean from the east, Alalakh (a little inland from the later Antioch) had already been the site of 15 cities, and its temple had been rebuilt and dedicated to different gods as many times. The names of the population were mostly Semitic, but in the mid-second millennium their ruling class was Mitannian.

Between the spheres of influence of Egypt and Mitanni, there was still an uneasy border zone of small Syrian city-states which sought to play off the one great power against the other. In the 16th century B.C., Egypt engulfed many of the coastal neighbors of Byblos, cities in the area later to be known as Phoenicia which were now heard of for the first time. But the most formidable reckoning for the minor Levantine states came a century later from the armies of Thothmes III.

The prince of Kadesh—a fortress which commanded the passage between Lebanon and Anti-Lebanon at the point where this route widens into the broad plains of north Syria—had instigated a confederacy to resist Thothmes. Kadesh was joined by a southerly city, Megiddo. Commanding the Jezreel (Esdraelon) gap which separates the hills of Galilee to the north from those of Judaea to the south, Megiddo was of such strategic importance that its name has earned a grim reputation in the form of Armageddon. But the Egyptians, operating by land and sea from their fortified base at Gaza, crushed the confederate armies beneath the walls of Megiddo itself. As the king of Egypt complained, they failed to take the city although "its capture is equal to the capture of a thousand cities," because they were so eager to pick up the plunder of the battlefield.

However, Megiddo fell three weeks later, and the insatiably aggressive Thothmes III seems ultimately to have conquered almost the whole of western Syria, placing its towns under vassal princelings and establishing, at the price of freedom, a unity of rule and communications which the area had never seen before and was not to see again for nearly a thousand years.

Much weakened by this Egyptian expansion in their southern flank, the Mitanni succumbed during the 14th century to a power which had arisen to their northwest in Asia Minor: the kingdom of the Hittites. Originating somewhere between the Carpathians and the Caucasus, these people had arrived in Asia Minor shortly before 2000 B.C., their migration forming part of that huge wave of assaults from the north which extended from India to western Europe and affected the destinies of the entire Near and Middle East. The Hittites cremated their dead, used iron—eventually smelting it into a metal stronger than bronze—and employed formidable horse chariots.

For three centuries Syria became a battleground between Hittites and Mitannians, until under Suppiluliumas I (*circa* 1380-40) the Hitties were wholly victorious. The prince of Byblos appealed desperately to Pharaoh Akhenaten of Egypt; but he was a visionary who did not concern himself with foreign affairs, and the numerous appeals were ignored.

One of the most important towns which was obliged to note the change of political wind was Ugarit (Ras Shamra, "fennel") on the north Syrian coast not far from the modern Latakia. Ugarit profited from its central position upon the trade routes to become one of the great ports of the Mediterranean. During its climax, between 1400 and 1200 B.C., it dispatched Mesopotamian, Hurrian, Hittite, Egyptian, Syrian, and Aegean products far and wide.

The city had very close links with Crete and other islands, and also with the Greek mainland where Mycenae had become a dominant power. Cretans and Mycenaeans had their own trading settlements at Ugarit, with separate living quarters and burial palaces in town and harbor. There were also groups of commercial travelers from other coastal cities, as well as from Cyprus and Egypt; a passport has been found authorizing a man and his son to use the routes to Egypt and Hittite territories. The manufactures and cultures of all these countries were on the move, and the center most largely responsible for their diffusion was Ugarit.

The royal palace, consisting of 70 rooms, five courtyards, a park and ornamental lake, also possessed a furnace for baking the clay tablets which scribes used to write on. These writings include not only the local government's extensive and varied records but at least four cycles of epic history, describing—in a western Semitic dialect akin to Hebrew—the exploits and rivalries of the gods with a diversity of subject matter which reflects the blend of the various racial and cultural elements at Ugarit.

The epics were written in a variation of the old wedge-shaped cuneiform script of Mesopotamia, which was in the process of being adapted to novel alphabetic purposes. Formerly each of these signs had represented a syllable, but this system was inconvenient since it needed far too many signs. From early in the second millennium, therefore, there had been Syrian experiments making them denote not only a whole syllable, as hitherto, but the first sounds of a syllable.

However, the old wedge-shaped imprints were only suitable for clay and stone, which were clumsy media, and by 1500 various places in Syria and Israel had instead taken the Egyptian pictorial, linear script and adapted it, radically, to the new sort of phonetic notation; and then the direction was moved from vertical to horizontal. And so, finally, a Byblos inscription of 1000 shows a real (though still vowel-less) alphabet. Writing had now become a very great deal easier to learn, and was accessible to enormously increased numbers of people.

However, in relation to the great powers of the day

—the Hittites and Egyptians—these Canaanite people were middlemen in the most literal and uncomfortable sense, sandwiched between the great powers. They finally clashed in around 1286 when Mutawallis the Hittite fought Rameses II of Egypt at Kadesh. Egyptian propaganda, already in those days very active, claimed a victory, but probably the Hittites really won. After further fighting, however, the two powers (unprecedentedly) made peace, fixing relative spheres of influence in Syria—which had, therefore, to stop its perilous tightrope trick of maintaining a precarious balance between the two empires.

But now furious onslaughts descended upon both sides from many backward peoples who were on the move over a vast area. Desperate emergencies which descended upon the Egyptians shortly before and after 1200 were in the end successfully fought off, though at a terrible cost, and Egypt was not, after all, engulfed. But the Hittite empire crumbled and collapsed—and in Syria, too, there was chaos. Excavations show that Aleppo, Carchemish, Alalakh, and Ugarit all fell to the invading hordes, and so did a whole series of recently emerged towns and fortresses of Judaea.

Who were the people who spread these massive devastations far and wide? There was a gigantic series of migratory waves extending all the way from the Danube valley to the plains of China. Their causes cannot be determined nor can it be confirmed whether, as has been suggested, drastic climatic changes played a part. Egyptian sources call the invaders Peoples of the Sea, and relate them to "the northern countries which are in their isles" or shorelands. The same records also refer to specific peoples or tribes, but their names, unfortunately, can be interpreted in a variety of ways. Probably they included dispossessed Anatolians and Aegeans; and swords, brooches, cremation rites, and probably also ships of European type now appear. The rocky southern coasts of Asia Minor, which had always served as nurseries and havens for pirates, are very likely to have been used as bases, and the invaders may well have been coastal peoples who had learned their techniques of warfare while serving the great powers as sailors and mercenary soldiers.

One of these Sea Peoples established itself at the lower extremity of the seaborad in present-day Israel. This was the tribe of the Philistines, who had finally come to occupy important positions in the Egyptian army and then, during the 12th century, subdued the Canaanite population throughout the coastal region between Mount Carmel and Gaza. The northern half of this strip was the Plain of Sharon, but it was the southern part, subsequently called Philistia, which contained the chief towns of their confederacy. The principal center seems to have been Ashdod, situated in a commanding position three miles from the sea, not above a harbor since there were only straight beaches in that area, but adjoining the road which led from Egypt and the Philistine border town, Gaza, up to the Sharon plain and Syria beyond.

The Philistines (whose name means "migrants" but now has an abusive significance because 19th-century German students called the non-University youth by this name) were a formidable people who during the mid-11th century B.C. temporarily reduced all their neighbors (including the Hebrews) to impotence. It was the Philistines, furthermore, who bequeathed to the Holy Land its historic name of Palestine.

One of the Hebrew prophets indicted that the Philistines had come originally from Caphtor—a term which, though it may cover various east Mediterranean areas, seems to refer particularly to Crete. The Philistines certainly possessed strong links with the Cretans and even stronger ones with the Mycenaeans. The distinctive wine jars of Philistia display a series of imitations of Mycenaean styles interpreted in local clays and techniques. The armor of the Philistines' champion Goliath was Aegean in character. Although nothing of their speech and script has survived except a few proper names, they seem to have spoken a language that was not Semitic like that of their Hebrew neighbors but Indo-European, or at least connected with that family of tongues. However, the Canaanites who became their subjects evidently exercised a reciprocal influence, since Philistine towns generally retained Canaanite names.

Their strength lay partly in their high-prowed ships, which are depicted by Egyptian artists, and partly also in horses and chariots—but principally in their use of iron which, under efficient monopolistic control, became a common, everyday metal. The Egyptians were impressed by the huge round shields and stout swords of the Philistines, and iron also began to be used for the tips of plows, which thus became better able to turn over the heavier soils where corn, vines, and olives were cultivated. A further new technical aid of a different sort consisted of the camel, which was domesticated in about the 12th century and inaugurated the great caravans from Philistia to Mesopotamia.

But behind this coastal area occupied by the Philistines lay the stretch of Judaean uplands into which groups of Hebrews, taking advantage of the widespread convulsions, gradually came from Egypt (where they had sojourned since the time of Joseph), apparently joining up with other tribes which they found in the region. According to recent research this Exodus is likely to have taken place in the 13th century B.C. (though it may have occurred somewhat earlier).

The Israel of Saul, David, and Solomon began two centuries later and this is the only part of the entire history of the Syria-Lebanon-Israel area which may be described as well known and does not need repeating here. But two facts are peculiarly significant to the present account. One of them is that the Jewish religion, which now took shape, was outstanding among all the heritages diffused from this area of many diffusions, outlasting *ad infinitum* the political background against which it grew. Secondly, the kingdom which reached its climax under Solomon (*circa* 974-937 B.C.) was more powerful than any which was ever formed in the Syria-Lebanon-Israel region throughout ancient times; and it has only been approached again, or equalled, by the Israel of A.D. 1967-8.

Jerusalem, enjoying a judicious blend of accessibility and isolation, dated back to around 2600 B.C., having been founded—as recent excavations show—on a site to the southeast of the Old City in order to guard an essential spring in the valley. The Canaanite tribe of the Jebusites, from whom David took over the city, had performed a major town-planning operation, and Solomon employed the resources of his coastal ally, Tyre, to endow it with a splendid temple. The excavation of 450 well-built horse-boxes at Megiddo, though of slightly later date, shows the Philistine-style chariotry on which he relied.

The further large-scale development of Philistine metal-working, too, is shown by finds at Ezion-geber near the northern end of the Gulf of Eilat, which have disclosed Solomon's elaborate, unique plants for the smelting and refining of copper and iron. In order to generate the maximum heat, these metal-works were situated at a place where the wind is strongest—and not too far away from woods which could supply the refinery with fuel. Both metals were amply exploited. At Cartan in the Jordan valley many bronze objects of the tenth century have been discovered, and the increased use of iron made for greater efficiency in agriculture. So, also, did a new and rapidly extended practice of lining cisterns with waterproof lime-plaster for the conservation and storage of rainwater.

Yet the political strength of the Hebrews rapidly declined because after Solomon it proved impossible to maintain national unity, and the country split into two parts. The ten northern tribes established a new dynasty to form the kingdom of Israel, which after two changes of capital established its royal residence at Samaria, a central observation point near the plains of Sharon and Jezreel. The single tribe of Judah, later enlarged by border rectifications, retained its capital at Jerusalem, under the house of David.

Both states flourished in the eighth century B.C.—Israel with a ruling class of aristocrats and wealthy merchants and Judah with a more homogeneous population. Neither kingdom was large or strong enough to exert independent political influence, or was even able for very long to survive. In 721 Samaria was conquered by the Assyrian king Sargon II. The more compact state of Judah held out until 597, but then Jerusalem succumbed to the Babylonian army of Nebuchadrezzar. A subsequent revolt was followed by two years' siege, at the end of which the city was captured and razed to the ground in 586.

Massive deportations, after each kingdom fell, led to the widespread dispersion which in due course spread the influence of the Jews, and the religion they so remarkably retained, throughout the Mediterranean area. Yet it was not long after the fall of Jerusalem that a partial return to their homeland began. Captivity ended when Persia, which had succeeded to Babylon's empire (539), allowed 42,000 Jews to go back to a small area around Jerusalem, and a new temple was built (516). Subsequent Mediterranean empires allowed or encouraged the existence of small local principalities of Hebrew faith, but it was not until the most modern times that a state comparable in strength with that of David and Solomon has been reestablished.

The north of Syria had remained outside their influence, and in other hands, and in the 13th century B.C., when everything was in a state of collapse, the downfall of the Hittites had caused a vacuum throughout Asia Minor. But throughout the peninsula's Mesopotamian and Syrian borderlands, Hittite influence though adulterated was not destroyed, and a network of small kingdoms formed a "strange Hittite afterglow" which lasted for nearly 500 years. These little states are often called "Neo-Hittite," but the Hittite-descended rulers only formed a veneer over populations containing complex racial mixtures in which the Canaanite strain predominated. The survival of the communities was due to the strength of their hilltop towns, which were often round or oval in shape and possessed massive walls, sometimes in two concentric circles.

Most of these states were based on centers in the interior of Syria, including Zincirli (Mt. Amanus), towns in the Amik plain (lower Orontes), and Hamath. Every minor principality of this kind was in constant danger from the Assyrians, but the spectacular invasions by the latter were punctuated by respites when they temporarily fell into political decline.

One of these setbacks, in the 12th century B.C., had been caused by yet another fresh wave of Semitic-speaking immigrants, the Aramaeans. The invasions and infiltrations of these originally uncouth nomads continued from the 14th century onwards for 200 years, a period when the whole of the eastern Mediterranean was suffering from upheavals.

Overwhelming Assyria and Babylonia, the Aramaeans broke shortly after 1200 into the central latitudes of Syria, where their tribes eventually consolidated into a series of small states which became neighbors and enemies of the Neo-Hittite kingdoms. At first the frontier between these two distinct and hostile groups passed south of Hamath through Lebanon, but then the Aramaeans struck north and conquered Hamath and Zincirli, so that in all Syria only the lower Orontes valley and its hinterland were left under Neo-Hittite control.

The Aramaeans were landsmen, skilled in caravan traffic and controling the trade routes from east to west and south to north which crossed in their territories. Yet these small states had no easier passage than their predecessors in a world of larger powers.

This was even true of the strongest of them, Damascus, situated beyond Anti-Lebanon—between Israel and Hamath—in a 30-mile-wide plain famous for its grainfields, orchards, gardens, and olive groves. The princes of Damascus had to look vigilantly in both directions. First they were obliged to contend with their momentarily powerful and, indeed, dominant Hebrew neighbors during the successive reigns of Saul, David and Solomon. Then Damascus became an ally of Israel and tried to resist the Assyrians, but the coalition it led against them in around 853 B.C. was defeated at Qarqar northwest of Hamath.

The next disastrous threat to the Aramaeans occurred during the following century, when many of their states became the vassals of a new power formed by the rulers of Urartu. These were a people of horsemen and herdsmen, perhaps speaking a language derived from the area of the Caucasus. They derived most of their art from Assyria but displayed peculiar expertise in metal work, engineering, and irrigation. The Urartian capital was far to the east on Lake Van, but they established protectorates over the Neo-Hittite territories along the lower Orontes valley and seacoast, and pushing south through Syria reduced a number of Aramaean principalities also.

At the end of the eighth century, however, the power of Urartu was broken by the Assyrians. These now proceeded to annex the Neo-Hittite kingdoms which the Urartians had controlled—before long we hear of a ruler in the Hatay being executed—while the Aramaean states resumed their efforts to maintain an independent existence. Sometimes they prospered, but it was not very long before Damascus and its allies succumbed finally to Tiglath-Pileser III of Assyria (*circa* 733), and soon afterwards a similar confederacy, under the leadership of Hamath, was again overwhelmed (*circa* 721).

Following the immemorial custom of the region the Aramaeans were not so much cultural innovators themselves as borrowers of elements from other people's cultures and religions. These borrowings included a simple practical script modified from Phoenician models. And yet, by a strange chance, it was these Aramaeans who were destined to impose their language upon the entire Near-Eastern world. By the time of Jesus, who himself spoke Aramaic, its dialect reigned unchallenged as the common speech of all Near-Eastern peoples.

On the coast to the west of Damascus, the great ports of Phoenicia were concentrated within easy reach of one another. Their Semitic-speaking inhabitants were Canaanites who had escaped absorption by the more recently arrived Aramaeans owing to the protection afforded by the limestone Lebanon massif, which rises steeply in the immediate hinterland. Certain passes, it is true, were inviting to enemies, notably at either extremity of the range the Litani (Leantes) and the Nahrel-Kelb (Eleutheros), of which the Hanles still bear the inscriptions of many invaders. Yet the passes brought not only occasional conquerors but also more frequent traders along the reopened camel-caravan routes.

And these gaps in the mountains, with their perennial streams, also brought down a more reliable supply of rainwater than the temporary rivers in between. With the help of this water, each community had its own strip of cultivable land, small but fertile enough to grow vines and olives and breed sheep, goats, and cattle. Nevertheless, the towns did not face landwards; from their two-way-facing harbors on bold headlands and adjoining islets, they looked out to sea.

In around 1100 Tiglath-Pileser I of Assyria extorted tribute not only from Byblos but also from two other cities, Sidon and Arvad (Arados). Sidon is 40 miles south of Byblos, Arvad 50 miles away to the north. This admission of suzerainty meant that, temporarily, the timber and other resources of the cities were in Assyrian hands. But during the period of great stress which followed, neither Assyria nor Egypt could maintain control, and Phoenicia had its chance.

To begin with, Byblos still exercised some sort of dominance over Sidon and Tyre, but before long both these cities in turn profited from the long maritime experience of the Byblians to take the lead themselves. The rise of Sidon ("Fishery") came suddenly in around 990-80 B.C. when the victories of the Israelites under David had neutralized the Aramaean peril in the hinterland. Tyre (Sur, "the Rock"), 20 miles from Sidon and separated from it by a gully, was called "its daughter." Probably this means that its population included Sidonian immigrants, in addition to sea-raider settlers and coastal Canaanites. As elsewhere in Phoenicia, tombs show mixtures of different kinds of burial rites.

Under David and Solomon, whose temple was built by Tyrians, these people took the lead, and for a time at least their king, Hiram I (*circa* 970-36), ruled Sidon as well. Air and submarine archaeology has revealed the partially submerged quays of Tyre, and the turrets and battlements of the town appear on an Assyrian relief. In the ninth and eight centuries trade continued to mount and multiply in the crowded many-storied houses of Tyre, "the crowning city," said Isaiah, "whose merchants are princes, whose traffickers are the honorable of the earth."

As in the most antique past, many of these cargoes consisted of the timber of Lebanon, to which the Old Testament refers in detail. But an even more important export consisted of clothing and textiles, colored with the dyes which Phoenicians extracted from the spiny-shelled *murex* (rock-whelk) caught in baskets off their coast.

Each *murex* secretes two precious drops of a yellowish liquid from which tones ranging from rose to dark violet could be extracted in the boiling vat. In the absence of mineral dyes, this was the only fast and firm dye the ancients possessed, not needing to be treated with the alum or fixatives which had to be added to vegetable colorings. The hills of shells on the outskirts of Tyre and Sidon (the refuse of factories located on the lee sides of the town owing to their unpleasant smell) recall the vast scale of the exploitation.

The inhabitants of this coast may well have owed their national name of dark or purple men (Phoinikes) to the lucrative monopoly which transformed their robes into these colors. They were also excellent weavers and embroiderers, and superb metallurgists, working and then exporting silver brought from Cilicia, and copper imported from Cyprus and refined with fuel from their own Lebanese hills. The Phoenicians were also famous for gold-working techniques of *repousse* and granulation which they had learned from Mycenae and Egypt. And from the Egyptians again they had mastered the art of converting their fine, flinty river sand into popular and exportable glass.

Like earlier peoples in this cultural melting pot, the Phoenicians gained their aesthetic ideas from a great number of sources. For example, their ivory work resembles the ivories produced in other parts of Syria (as well as by Syrians working in Israel and Assyria) in its facile synthesis of Egyptian, Canaanite, Aramaean, and Cypriot models into neat and delicate masterpieces—

which in turn gave many ideas to the Greeks.

An even stronger influence was exercised by the Phoenician and Syrian alphabet which before about 800—serving a literature of which we have little knowledge—developed from Canaanite models into a mature form which only needed the addition of vowels (by the Greeks) to turn into the alphabet used by the ancient Indo-European speaking peoples from whom we ourselves derive our writing.

The maritime enterprise of the Phoenicians exceeded even that of the far-ranging Mycenaeans. They are said to have been the first people to navigate by observing the stars, to travel beyond the sight of land, to sail at night, and to undertake voyages in wintertime. Representations have survived showing their trading ships with curved prows and sterns and two banks of oars below a raised deck.

Since, unlike the Egyptians, they had no great river to serve as a navigation school, for them it was the open Mediterranean, sink or swim; no shelter was available nearer than Cyprus, which developed through their colonization a strange, fantastic culture, part Phoenician and part Mycenaean. The Phoenicians extended the great Mycenaean heritage of exploration, trading, and colonization throughout the Mediterranean. Most notable of all was their establishment of Carthage (*circa* 814) which diffused the ideas and institutions of Tyre and Sidon in many parts of the west, and only finally succumbed to Rome nearly 700 years later.

But the recovery of Assyria in the ninth century B.C., which brought heavy pressure upon the Neo-Hittite and Aramaean states, bore heavily upon the Phoenicians as well. Tyre and Sidon were among the cities which bowed before the storm and paid successive Assyrian monarchs their tribute of gold, silver, fine many-colored cloths, and ivory.

They also had to accept Assyrian governors (around 742), and although still allowed to fell timber in the Lebanon, they were taxed when it was brought down to the warehouses. This provoked riots, but Sargon II "gave peace" to Tyre; Sennacherib like others used its sailors; and Esarhaddon (68–69) laid waste rebellious Sidon, and allowed artists to represent him holding the prince of Tyre (as well as the king of Egypt) upon a leash.

Assyria's position, however, began to weaken when its neighbors the Medes, in what is now northwestern Persia, asserted their independence in about 620. Soon afterwards, they jointly attacked and destroyed the Assyrian capital Nineveh. Their allies in this enterprise were the Babylonians, who took over the Assyrian heritage and drove out an Egyptian army which had again penetrated from end to end of the Levant.

This victory, at Carchemish, was won by the king's son Nebuchadrezzar, who during his own subsequent reign captured not only Jerusalem but then Tyre, which fell after a seige of 13 years (*circa* 571). Sidon, which apparently gave in without a struggle, was restored to its ancient position as the chief town in Phoenicia.

A quarter of a century later, the overthrow of Babylon by the Persians brought to an end the vast phase of Near Eastern history which had been dominated by Mesopotamia (Sumeria, Assyria, Babylonia). Yet, Sidon and Tyre still displayed greater powers of survival than their masters, for although they too passed into the Persian empire for more than two centuries, they continued to provide the conquerors with their seamen and their fleets.

The period in ancient history when there were independent states in Syria and Israel had gone forever. But their contribution to the history of the Mediterranean, through the Mediterranean to our own development, had been gigantic. The same circumstances which had brought countless invasions, immigrations, and infiltrations down upon these lands had filled them with a vast variety of cultures. And the next thing that happened was that these diverse cultural influences spread extensively toward the west.

This was partly due to the seafaring of the Phoenicians and their colony of Carthage. But it was also due to the fact that the Greeks, at the most formative stage of their cultural and artistic development (eighth-seventh centuries B.C.), had just re-established contact with Syria, particularly through their commercial settlement at Al Mina (Posidium); and the Greeks drew an immense amount of inspiration from what they learned in that area. Admittedly they transformed what they learned in an inspired fashion all their own.

All the same, it was this territory of Syria-Lebanon-Israel which had provided the basis for Greek cultural development. Greek "orientalizing" art (and its Etruscan offshoot in Italy) is full of modified Neo-Hittite and Syrian and Phoenician themes, and Assyrian and Urartian and Babylonian motifs that had come through Syria.

It was also from Syria and Phoenicia that the Greeks borrowed many of their myths and learned their alphabet; and it was through these countries again that the Hellenistic monarchies learned the systems and organizations of the great Mesopotamian monarchies of the past, and handed on this knowledge to Rome. And it was along the roads and sea routes of Rome that the outstanding religious creations of this same area, Jewish monotheism and Christianity, spread over the western world. Our debt to the nameless, explosive rectangle of territory which includes Israel, Lebanon, and Syria is incalculable.

The Egyptian and Hittite clash at Kadesh circa
1286 B.C.

Christ crucified

CHRISTIANITY: FROM HUNTED SECT TO STATE RELIGION

By Michael Grant

*I*t was a long time before the authorities in Rome and the numerous provinces of its vast empire clearly distinguished Christianity from its Jewish parent body. Although the Romans had apparently seen some difference between the two faiths as early as Nero's persecution of A.D. 64—the traditional date of the martyrdoms of St. Peter and St. Paul—the tendency persisted to treat Christians as an extremist branch of Judaism.

But if the Jews enjoyed a certain guarded tolerance because they were following their ancestral national religion, there was felt to be no such excuse for the Christians. Besides, the appeal of Christianity to slaves and other poor people, and its promises of a classless salvation, could be interpreted as subversive, especially in times of national emergency.

Indeed, Greco-Roman society felt provoked by the

whole way of life of the Christian communities. Without even the Jewish justification of a national sect and custom, they too lived apart, worshipped apart, considered themselves chosen, and set up values and standards opposed to those normally and traditionally correct.

Even after the initial belief in an immediate Second Coming had waned, their instructions were to love not the world, neither the things that are in the world, but to consider themselves as strangers and sojourners. Many a thoughtful pagan of the time had similar convictions, but it is easy to see how they could result in mass outbursts of violence against the Christians who, as the historian Tacitus pointed out, seemed like the Jews to "hate the human race."

And yet for another century or more the Roman emperors, concerned as always to lower the temperature, were more inclined to protect Christians from the hostile public than to convict them of any crime. A request for guidance from Pliny the Younger, Governor of Pontus and Bithynia in northern Asia Minor, was answered by Trajan (A.D. 98-117) with the ruling that they were not to be hunted out.

"Any who are accused and convicted should be punished, but if a man says he is not a Christian and makes this obvious by his conduct—*namely by worshipping our gods*—then his second thoughts should earn him pardon." Since the attitude of the Christians was held to be an offense against the state religion, this was a remarkable privilege.

Nevertheless penalties were enforced from time to time, principally when concessions to popular agitation seemed desirable. Thus under the otherwise enlightened Marcus Aurelius (A.D. 161-80), the Gallic population became hostile to the oriental Christian businessmen in the Rhone and Saone valleys, and the peoples of Gaul and Asia Minor, and then North Africa, rioted

CHRISTIANITY: FROM HUNTED SECT TO STATE RELIGION

against the Christians as scapegoats for military, economic, and natural disasters.

There were arrests and sadistic executions, and one of the victims was Polycarp, Bishop of Smyrna. Yet at his trial he pointed out that Christians were taught to render honor, "if it hurt us not, to princes and authorities appointed by God." For there was also a widely held belief among members of the faith that the simultaneous appearance of the Saviour and of the Imperial Peace, created by Augustus, had not been fortuitous.

All the same, the philosopher Celsus delivered a full-scale attack on the Christians at about this time (? c. 177-8). Why, he asked, do they not play their part in public life? If everyone took such an uncooperative line, there would soon be an end of everything sensible and every kind of religion including theirs.

The controversy had begun. Christians were accused of obscenity and cannibalism, and Tatian from Syria retaliated by telling of pagans who ate Christian flesh to prevent its resurrection. It was also perhaps then that Minucius Felix wrote the first extant defense of Christianity in Latin, a mild, philosophical affair very different from the fiery works of Tertullian which were to follow.

They were provoked by the first coordinated, empire-wide sanctions against the Christians. These were launched by Septimius Severus (193-211), who subjected all converts to Christianity (as well as Judaism) to severe penalties. An impetuous, argumentative, learned North African, Tertullian devoted his flashing, scathing Latin not to conciliation, but to aggressive attacks on the defiled tongues and filthy sacrificial offerings of the heathen, who would themselves, he added, become the victims of a far more frightful holocaust on the Day of Judgment. Tertullian moved gradually from temporal loyalty to total non-cooperation with the authorities.

CHRISTIANITY: FROM HUNTED SECT TO STATE RELIGION

The measures of Severus were followed by a period of tolerance. When Origen, the greatest product of the Alexandrian school which tried to philosophize Christianity, wrote his refutation of the attacks by Celsus, he knew that further terrible upheavals were coming. He asserted that Christians should pray for the emperor, if he was a good emperor, and for the imperial cause if there was a just war, but that Christ is stronger than the emperor, all his officers, and the whole senate and people of Rome.

Christian communities, though still small, were now efficiently organized. Oligarchic and democratic tendencies had been shelved in favor of government by bishops, who paid their priests from a central bank and could stand up to imperial and municipal bureaucrats. The precedents set by Jewish charities and Greco-Roman mutual assistance projects were developed and expanded into Christian welfare measures that were much wider in scope, looking after old people and widows, the poor and oppressed, and victims of the plague and other sicknesses.

This was one of the consequences of the very nature of Christianity. For although love of one's neighbor was found in other faiths, this was the only religion to profess and practice total, revolutionary, unrestricted love, charity, compassion and consolation, without distinction of birth, sex, occupation, race or education.

Even pagans admired Christian social services, but in times of trouble this compact state within a state seemed a provocation. And so the emperor Decius for the first time launched a serious persecution (250-251). He did not ask Christians to give up their religion, but singled out their leaders and would not tolerate refusals to join in communal corporate observances.

Decius was a soldier, and this was a soldier's order. It was also a psychological gesture intended to find someone to blame and to distract attention from gener-

CHRISTIANITY: FROM HUNTED SECT TO STATE RELIGION

al misery at a time of economic deterioration and disasters on the frontiers.

The emperor required every Christian to make just one pagan religious performance, for which he was given a Certificate of Sacrifice by his local Sacrificial Commission; specimens have been found in the all-preserving sands of Egypt. There were temporary renegades; those who refused to collaborate were put to death.

Martyrdoms rebounded on the authorities, because they were deeply admired by other Christians. The martyrs were convinced that they alone would be in Paradise until the Second Coming and that their sacrifice, founded upon Christ's, would speed the reconciliation between God and his people. The faithful threw their clothes on the places of execution, to soak up the blood of those who perished. "Where their bones are buried, devils flee as from fire and unbearable torture!" And the fact that Christianity had been found worth dying for made it seem worth living for as well. The most important shrine in Christendom was at the place in Rome where the first martyr, St. Peter, was believed to have his tomb.

Soon afterwards Valerian launched a new antichristian plan (257). The patriotic appeal was repeated, but since a financial crisis was at its height, what he really wanted was church property and he seized it at the same time as he banished the bishops. But his son reversed this policy, and during the forty years of toleration which then followed, Christianity became much more solidly established.

At the Carthage Council of 256 there were 87 North African bishops; fifty years later their number was probably trebled. Asia Minor was the country where the religion had first made great advances, but all over the southern and eastern Mediterranean, and especially where there was a noticeable Jewish or Semitic element, the balance was shifting slowly but perceptibly in this direction. The Christians were growing together with Greco-Roman society and were particularly strong among the shopkeepers, sailors, clerks, small traders, artisans and laborers of the towns.

At Rome, where the church continued to use the Greek language until the third century, there may have been about ten thousand Christians in A.D. 200, rising to thirty or forty thousand a century later and perhaps to twice the latter figure under Constantine.

Meanwhile, however, the most formidable of all theoretical attacks upon the basis of Christianity was launched by Porphyry (died c. 305), chief pupil of Plotinus who founded the Neo-Platonic school of philosophy. Less concerned than his predecessors with Roman patriotic motives, Porphyry, the leading orientalist of antiquity, concentrated on higher criticism designed to demolish the scriptures.

His Neo-Platonist collegue, Hierocles, then became one of the principal instigators of the Great Persecution which now followed (AD. 303-13.) Diocletian and his assistant emperor (Caesar) Galerius, who launched this onslaught, were strong religious conservatives, aiming at nothing less than the annihilation of the Christians.

This was a death struggle of faith against faith, of the old order against the new. The first of a series of edicts forbade all assemblies of Christians for purposes of worship and ordered the destruction of their churches and sacred books. Known adherents were dismissed from state employment, including the army in which emperor-cult was a requirement of military discipline. Then followed two further proclamations, limited in operation to the eastern provinces. These were directed solely against the clergy; one edict ordered their arrest and the other commanded that they should sacrifice to the gods of the state.

Resistance was unprecedentedly resolute and de-

CHRISTIANITY: FROM HUNTED SECT TO STATE RELIGION

fiant, and a considerable number of people were executed, particularly in eastern regions where Christianity was strongest, such as Egypt and the Levant. Diocletian, after a serious illness, abdicated (305), but the persecutions went on. It is impossible to say how many perished, perhaps about three thousand.

As these final bloody acts of the great tragedy ran their course, it became clear that the persecution had spent itself. Times had changed. The pagan communities no longer egged on the authorities with the same ferocity. On the contrary, they now regarded the victimization as exaggerated. The Christians, who were not so eccentric as they used to be, seemed rather less unlikable than the government, which was now totalitarian and terrorized the entire population.

And so, in circumstances which still remain obscure, Diocletian's successor in the eastern provinces, Galerius, on his deathbed, issued an edict granting freedom of worship to all members of the Christian faith (311).

"Persecution," declared the dying emperor, "had only made them obstinate or caused them to cease worshipping any god at all. So in view of our benevolence and the established custom by which we invariably grant pardon to all men, we have thought proper in this matter also to extend our clemency most gladly, so that Christians may again exist and rebuild the houses in which they used to meet, on condition that they do nothing contrary to public order. In view of this our clemency, they are in duty bound to beseech their own god for our security, and that of the state and of themselves, in order that in every way the state may be preserved in health and they may be able to live free from anxiety in their own homes."

That is to say, for the first time in history, the Christians were given a measure of legal recognition. Nor did this edict merely allow them to exist; by enjoining them to pray for emperor and state it implicitly recognized their God as a divine power. Nothing definite was said about church property, but Galerius' rival at Rome, Maxentius (306-12), although himself a devoted adherent of patriotic cults, restored to the church whatever property had been confiscated during the persecutions.

In the east, however, Maximinus II Daia, who had now succeeded Galerius, fought a strong rear-guard action against the encroachments of Christianity. He had at first grudgingly accepted the edict of Galerius, but then his attitude changed and persecution began again. Petitions were conveniently received from the municipal authorities at Nicomedia and Tyre and from provincial organizations requesting that their Christian residents should be expelled, and Daia graciously agreed.

"If they persist in their damnable folly, let them be thrown out as you requested, and driven right away from your city and neighborhood, in order that thereby, in accordance with your praiseworthy enthusiasm in this matter, your city may be purged of all contamination and impiety, and in pursuit of its set purpose may with due reverence give itself to the regular worship of the immortal gods. We permit your Dedicatedness to ask whatever munificence you wish in return for this your devout purpose. The fact of its being granted to your city will provide evidence for all time of your devoted piety towards the immortal gods."

To encourage this repressive action Maximinus Daia obtained and circulated confessions from prostitutes that they had taken part in Christian orgies. He also directed that spurious antichristian Acts of Pilate should be included in school curricula. Executions took place, but they were few, for Maximinus preferred tortures to death penalties in order to improve his statistics of apostasy; the obstinate were blinded in one eye and had one leg hamstrung and were then sent to mines and quarries.

But what interested Daia more than such penal measures was the positive establishment of a pagan organization which would rival and outdo its efficient Christian counterpart. And so he created an elaborate, homogenous, pagan ecclesiastical system with its own priestly hierarchy.

While this was happening in the eastern provinces the young Constantine the Great—of Illyrian origin like Decius and Diocletian—defeated Maxentius at the battle of the Milvian Bridge outside Rome and became sole master of the west (312). Constantine was in the midst of a determined but rather confused transition from sun worship, which with its grandiose simplicity had momentarily been adopted as the last official version of paganism, to the Christian faith.

Later in life he told the ecclesiastical historian Eusebius that, while marching in Gaul some time before his conquest of Italy, he had seen a cross of light superimposed upon the sun, with the injunction to "conquer with this sign" written in stars about the cross. What he saw may have been a rare natural phenomenon in which the sun's rays looked like a cross. Or it may have been one of the trance-like experiences with which the age abounded.

But whether it was the one or the other, or a combination of both, or a divine revelation, the vision stimulated the remarkable boldness that Constantine showed in his successful campaign against Maxentius. And it was also reported by the Christian writer Lactantius that before the Milvian Bridge the victorious emperor was warned in a dream to inscribe the monogram XP (*Christos*) upon his soldiers' shields.

In the east, Constantine had two co-rulers to deal with—Maximinus Dais in the non-European part of the empire and his rival Licinius (a friend of the late Galerius) in the Danubian provinces. Professing friendly relations with both, Constantine requested Daia to stop the persecution of the Christians and gave Licinius his half sister in marriage. At the wedding celebrations he and Licinius, in the so-called "Edict of Milan," came to an agreement about issuing a universal command introducing complete religious tolerance.

Constantine then left Maximinus Daia and Licinius to fight it out (313). Daia, defeated, agreed to a tolerant policy just before his death, and Licinius remained emperor of the east as Constantine's colleague for another eleven years. On the eve of his decisive battle against Maximinus, he also had claimed to have seen an angelic vision. But it was not explicitly Christian, nor was the monotheistic litany which his troops recited three times before the engagement; this was addressed to the Highest Holy God.

On Constantine's side, too, there was still much vague mention of the supreme godhead. But before long he explicitly identified the Divine Power with Jesus, spoke of "the lawful and most holy Christian religion" and initiated, over a period of years, a series of measures openly granting favor to the Christians. Their priests, other than those of dissident sects, were exempted from municipal obligations like those of the Jews.

But a more decisive step had already been taken when funds, presaging a heavy drain upon the national exchequer, were sent to subsidize provincial churches, for example at Carthage. The bishop of Rome (Pope) was given the royal palace of the Laterani and magnificent new churches. The liturgy borrowed imposing features from official and court ceremonial.

Moreover, the church, in keeping with its new privileges, was entrusted with public responsibilities. In spite of the differences between Christian ideas and pagan juristic traditions, episcopal courts were given

CHRISTIANITY: FROM HUNTED SECT TO STATE RELIGION

jurisdiction in civil cases (318). People were permitted to bequeath their property to the church, which thus ranked as a civic corporation. Finally Constantine himself was baptized, after postponing this like many other Christians, until his deathbed—when he could sin no more.

Church and state were to be run in double harness. But as the emperor became increasingly aware of his personal Mission, the successive Councils of Arelate (Arles) (314) and Nicaea (Iznik) (325)—the former attended by western and the latter mainly by eastern bishops—showed that the master was Constantine.

The celestial will, it was pointed out, had committed to him the government of all things on earth. Consequently membership of the church now meant resignation to the claims of the state, and an extremely oppressive state it was. Since, however, there was going to be an official church, nothing but this enforced subordination could produce the power structure needed to guarantee that state and church, and the empire with them, would not fall apart.

Eusebius, whose life of Constantine framed the new theory of Christian sovereignty in terms comparing the relationship of God with Jesus to that of Jesus with the emperor, felt so anxious not to return to the failings of earlier Christian institutions—whose persecution by Diocletian even seemed to him merciful—that he applauded the capitulation of the church to Constantine. St. Jerome (d. 420), on the other hand, felt that "as the Church increased its influence it decreased in Christian virtues."

And St. Augustine, bearing in mind the severities and brutalities of Constantine's regime, could not fully accept Eusebius' eulogy of that ruler, reserving unqualified praise for his own contemporary monarch Theodosius I (d. 395). It remained for St. Ambrose to introduce a new era of intrepid churchmen by rebuking

CHRISTIANITY: FROM HUNTED SECT TO STATE RELIGION

Theodosius. Constantine, too, had been requested by his chief religious adviser Hosius of Corduba not to interfere in ecclesiastical affairs, but his church did not seriously attempt to compete with the emperor, who was the author of its revolutionary transformation.

Constantine or his advisors may also have experienced a growing conviction that Christianity was the only force which could effectively bring together the conflicting social elements of the empire. Nevertheless, this conversion of the state was a rash and remarkable personal venture—one of the apocalyptic acts of history which deny the modern doctrine that everything happens impersonally through tendencies.

A tendency towards the spread of Christianity had, it is true, existed, but on too small a scale to exercise great effects without vigorous impulsion from above. At Rome the Christian population, although larger than before, still numbered as has been seen or more than seventy or eighty thousand, and relatively few of these people were of political or social significance. The empire became Christian because of the unlikely emergence of a Christian emperor. For this decisive Peace of the Church largely came about because of the private workings of the powerful, emotional personality of Constantine. In his heart he felt an impulsive, exalted need for divine support.

There was nothing very new about this. The third century A.D. had been a time when the whole Roman world, or at least its more thoughtful elements, had veered over from classical materialism to spiritual and indeed monotheistic preoccupations. The ambition of everyone was for salvation in the next world, and for the religion in this world which would ensure that immortality.

Paganism offered a vast variety of faiths that aimed to satisfy such cravings, including particularly the Mystery Religions of Demeter, Dionysus, Isis, Cybele, and

CHRISTIANITY: FROM HUNTED SECT TO STATE RELIGION

Mithra. If you were progressively initiated into the secrets of these cults, they claimed that you would be saved. Christianity said the same about its own faith, but why did it so decisively prevail in the mind of Constantine? Not only because of its efficient organization, doctrine of love and social services, but because its Saviour gave the most satisfying promise of all. For He was no myth like the others; He had actually lived—in the world of Rome—at a known time and place. And so there was a special alluring immediacy about the pathos and drama of His stay, and His offer to mankind was irresistible.

Nevertheless Constantine did not become a thoroughgoing Christian all at once. As his coins show, he passed through a phase of the sun worship which recent emperors had been stressing as the pagan solution to contemporary yearnings. There was much to be said for venerating this obvious giver of life. Yet such a faith wholly lacked the compulsive humanity of the worship of Christ.

Without a Christian ruler on the throne, and a singularly forceful and determined one at that, the conversion of the Roman world, if it had ever happened at all, would have taken a very long time. For example, the great Persian empire which was Rome's eastern neighbor, though its population included many Christians, never had a Christian monarch and consequently never became a Christian state.

The vast majority of Constantine's subjects were still pagans, and he insisted in the interests of unity that his Mission was not only for Christians, but that he was also bishop of those outside the church. Towards these pagans, still firmly entrenched in important positions, his attitude gradually underwent a predictable change. At first he proposed to "let those who are in error be free to enjoy the same peace and tranquility as those who believe."

CHRISTIANITY: FROM HUNTED SECT TO STATE RELIGION

They were, it is true, required to recite a general monotheistic prayer, and pagan terminology was gradually abolished from official vows. But only a few well-known heathen temples were closed down, and in two cases this action was ascribed to their unacceptable practice of ritual prostitution. However, the violent antipagan tone of Lactantius' *Deaths of the Persecutors* (c. 316) suggested that co-existence could not last for long.

When Licinius, in the east, became irritated by ecclesiastical disputes and reintroduced sanctions against the Christians in general (320-321), his relations with Constantine became strained, and the latter retaliated by showing increased hostility to the pagans. In the year of Licinius' downfall (324), Constantine passed a severe law against divination. In the eastern regions, which Constantine now added to his western realm, there were in future few provincial governors who did not belong to the Christian faith. Temple treasures were confiscated (331), and finally pagan sacrifices were banned.

Nevertheless it did take two more generations for all this pressure to deal paganism its death blow. Meanwhile, the pagans presented a less intractable and ominous problem to Constantine than disobedient fellow Christians. In 314 he wrote to a high official in North Africa that divine favor was only procurable by united worship, which should rise above quarrels and contentions distasteful to the Highest God. The Church must not only be united with the emperor; it was also imperative that Christians should be united with one another. As Eusebius pointed out, disharmony was a direct invitation to divine chastisement—nothing angers God so much as divisions in the church, which are the cutting up of the body of Christ.

Constantine's ecumenism was not a defensive closing of the ranks, like its modern counterpart, but a universal missionary attack launched at a time when he had boldly estimated that the tide was running in Christianity's favor. Moreover, unlike most modern ecumenists, Constantine (as King James I of England appreciatively noted) was influenced by a political motive. For heretical and schismatical deviations, besides calling down the wrath of God, would also, by opposing and disobeying the official church which was Constantine's own instrument, create communal anarchy and chaos and consequently thwart the imperial will.

Nevertheless, these tendencies were also lurking nearer home, for Constantine's unification of state and church did not please everyone. At the Council of Arles there was still a feeling that to serve the emperor was hardly compatible with membership of the church. The assembled clerics finally decided to the contrary, but it had indeed required a mental and spiritual turnabout to belong to a church which, instead of being perpetually proscribed, was subsidized and directed from the Lateran palace under the guidance of the emperor. St. Jerome's doubts about the desirability of such a situation echoed a feeling of disquiet that went wide and deep.

This feeling had ancient roots. Before official recognition of the church, many Christian writers had detested not only the Roman state but the whole Greco-Roman and particularly Greek philosophical culture in which the Alexandrian and other Apologists had tried to dress the Jewish doctrines of Christianity. Tertullian became a convert to one of the most extreme of these opposition cults, Montanism, which had come to Africa from the apocalyptic, penitential churches of Asian villages. This sort of Protestant attitude spread through the rural areas of Asia, Syria and North Africa.

Hitherto Christianity had always been mainly urban, and its extension to country areas raised new problems. The peasantry, although they provided the bulk of the empire's income, had always been totally subordinate to town dwellers and there was a complete lack of sympathy between the two. To the rustic populations, therefore, Christianity meant not only staunch hatred of the imperial persecutors, but social discontent and impatience, a general dislike of the establishment and savage disapproval of their fellow Christians in the towns. These rustic converts disliked city Christianity because it was increasingly formalized, institutionalized, and centralized and because its growing official hierarchy, in the interests of unity and peaceful progress, accepted too many compromises—in their view improper and deplorable compromises—with a sophisticated world.

Tertullian's harsh eloquence contains a strongly Semitic revulsion, Punic as well as Jewish, away from Rome and Greek attitudes towards a burning desert fundamentalism which inherited the supporters of fierce local pagan cults. This is a backward plunge to a naive prophetic church of puritanical austerity, basing itself on the Word of God, enthusiastically loathing the world and yearning for the martyr's crown. Christianity in northern Africa had never stressed love and mercy very strongly. Certainly Montanism did not. On the contrary, it was far more concerned with divine wrath and the terror of Judgment. The basis of salvation, said Tertullian, is fear.

A major breach between these puritans and the main Christian churches was caused by persecutions. When each wave of pressure ended, the churches tended to accept temporary renegades back into the fold. The more austere sects (most of them in rustic areas which had not felt the pressure so severely) parted company with them over this. Donatists in North Africa and Melitians in Egypt were still asserting these protests when Constantine instituted an official Christian church.

The dissenters, however, continued to dissent; indeed they completely denied not only the sovereignty of the church but all traditional, humanist, urban culture. Constantine excluded them from his subsidies, irrevocable positions were adopted, and the Donatists asked the new and crucial question of the day: What has the emperor to do with the Church?

Constantine's patience, exemplary at first though not strong by nature, gave way and he acted against them. Soon he relapsed into a scornful tolerance, but the damage had been done; the founder of the official church had instituted the terrible tradition of Christianity persecuting Christians. Meanwhile, persecution only strengthened the Donatists—and they had laid down the Protestant principles which re-emerged in full stature twelve hundred years later.

Another fundamental breach in the unity aimed at by Constantine did not have to wait so long to take effect, since it already became highly apparent, not in the sixteenth century but in the fifth and sixth. This was the rupture between the Catholic Church centered upon Rome and the Orthodox Church based on Constantinople. And this division, too, though it had perhaps already become inevitable by the time of Constantine, was hastened by one of his actions, namely the refoundation of Byzantium as Constantinople, the new capital of the empire (324-330). This city was far better situated than Rome (where emperors had not often resided in recent years) owing to its position on the main road between the Danube and Euphrates frontiers, at the point where this road was bisected by the maritime channel between the Mediterranean and Black Seas.

At the time when this foundation was being planned the Council of Nicaea declared Rome, Alexandria, and Antioch to be patriarchal sees. The Roman church, fatefully located in the imperial capital, had long enjoyed particular respect. Already in the second century Irenaeus put forward its superior claims on grounds of a direct chain of authority extending from St. Peter (chief apostle of Jesus) and St. Paul to bishops of his own day.

Eastern churches admitted Rome's special distinction, but they were very much more reluctant to admit that Rome had any right to legislate for them on doctrine or organization. They did not share the increasing western tendency to eliminate laymen from church government. It was also their belief that ecclesiastical authority was not vested in any one person, but belonged by scriptural direction to each bishop (in spite of "precedence of honeur" to a few holders of historic sees) and expressed itself through all of them united in their general councils.

Romans and Greeks never had much sympathy for one another's qualities, and as bilingual scholars became much rarer misunderstandings abounded. A quarrel over the celebration of Easter impelled the Roman bishop (Pope) St. Victor (died 199) to break with all churches of Asia Minor, and St. Stephen (254-256) was prompted by a dispute regarding baptism to insist on the subordination of all churches to Rome. This claim was denied by the easterner Firmilian of Caesarea.

For the Greeks could not share the legal, centralized training and the juristic molding which their faith had received from lawyers such as Tertullian. Nor did the Romans, for their part, appreciate the Hellenic philosophizing tendencies which were so strong in Greek lands. The east, said Milman, enacted creeds; the west, discipline.

These differences were accentuated and perpetuated by Constantine's foundation of Constantinople. The residence of earlier imperial governments away from Rome had already given the head of the Roman church far greater opportunities for independence and civil authority than he had possessed hitherto. But the presence of the emperor at Constantinople began to raise the patriarch of that city also to a peculiar importance of his own, which was later recognized by a precendence second only to Rome (381). Already the new city had been described, two decades earlier, by St. Gregory of Nazianzus as "a bond of union between east and west to which the most distant extremes from all sides come together, and to which they look up as the common center and emporium of the faith."

But Rome did nothing of the kind; St. Gregory proved too optimistic in view of the disputes which were to follow. They were concerned with clerical celibacy, the Fall of Man, and the nature of the Holy Ghost. The east as always stressed the singleness of the supreme diety; the west emphasized the divinity of Jesus. Constantinople as the imperial capital had sharpened longstanding cultural, psychological, and linguistic differences.

The result was not the religious unity for which Constantine had hoped, but a major breach between Catholicism and Orthodoxy which has lasted until now—though efforts are at last being made to bridge the gulf as they are also being made to heal that other major breach, also in part due to Constantine's actions, which foreshadowed the creation of separate Protestant churches. The effect of Constantine's ecumenical drive was, paradoxically, not unity but permanent Christian division, productive of all the weakness of disunion and all the vigor of separate militant loyalties.

Trajan

ITALICA: THE ROMANS IN SPAIN

By Sylva E. Mularchyk

*D*own through history, the people of the peninsula now called Spain have known many conquerors and survived many upheavals. The earliest evidence of mankind inhabiting Spain is found in cave paintings, such as those so beautifully preserved in the caverns of Altamira in Santander province, which were executed about twenty thousand years before the birth of Christ during the Paleolithic Age. These paintings, discovered only a hundred years ago, and others like them, have given us a wonderful glimpse into the lives of those primitive hunters, only shortly removed from the beasts whose caves they shared.

Numerous artifacts left by the Neolithic peoples and those of the later metal ages have also been found, from which man's progress is clearly discernible. Dur-

ITALICA: THE ROMANS IN SPAIN

ing the Iron Age, in the eleventh century B.C., the Phoenicians first crossed the Mediterranean Sea in search for tin and touched the shores of Spain. They were well rewarded, for the land was rich in precious metals of all kinds, and for several centuries the Phoenicians carried off the wealth of the peninsula. It was said that they plated the anchors and iron fittings of their ships with gold and silver so that more could be taken away.

About 1000 B.C., the Celts first entered Spain through the Pyrenees Mountains, coming down from the northern lands. In the sixth century B.C., the Greeks came to colonize Spain, finding a race of people which they called the Iberians. These were a Caucasoid race who had probably originated in Asia and had crossed over into Africa and then to Spain some centuries earlier. Stone structures or cairns of the Neolithic Age have been found in Spain and are attributed to the early Iberians.

This indigenous civilization was made up of many tribes, such as the Tartessians, Mastienians, and the Lusitanians, and for a long time they warred against the Celtic tribes; but eventually both the Celts and the Iberians, considering the peninsula "Hispania" their native land, found it expedient to join forces against the foreign invaders, such as the Phoenicians, Greeks, and the Carthaginians who had also arrived about the sixth century B.C. From the two vastly different cultures of the fair-skinned Celt and the swarthier Iberian, emerged the hardy Celt-Iberian, forerunner of the present-day Spaniard.

During the centuries while Greece and Carthage were relieving Spain of her rich ores, without much effort at colonization, the Roman Empire was in its infancy. According to tradition, Rome was founded in 753 B.C. by the twin Romulus. By the fifth century B.C., Rome had become an important republic, increas-

ITALICA: THE ROMANS IN SPAIN

ing its power, its rulers determined to conquer the entire known world—a desire it came close to fulfilling, for during the first century of the Christian era, Rome's empire covered Italy, Greece, Spain, France, the Netherlands, Britain, part of Germany, and some portions of Western Asia and Northern Africa.

In the second Punic War, which raged between Rome and Carthage from 218 B.C. to 202 B.C., the Roman General Publio Scipio Africanus overthrew Hannibal, who led the Carthaginian forces. The victorious Romans took possession of the naval base at Nova Cartago (Cartagena) and continued their expansion throughout Hispania. Other important strongholds along the Mediterranean coast were Saguntum (Sagunto) and Tarraco (Tarragona). The Romans lost no time in moving inland, their purpose being not only to conquer but also to colonize. In the southwest, in 206 B.C., after the battle of Ilipa (Alcala del Rio), they took the lands sloping north of the Betis River (now Guadalquivir) and the entire valley, except Gades (Cadiz), which fell later.

The Celt-Iberians were formidable warriors as well as wily and disturbing enemies who often changed sides. It took the Romans two centuries to subdue the scattered and stubborn tribes, although much of the region known as Baetica (later to be called Andalusia after the onslaught of the Vandals) was soon Romanized. It remained and prospered under Roman rule and influence about four hundred years. The lands of Baetica were rich and fertile, and Roman settlers moved in quickly.

Baetica was a part of Ulterior Spain, one of the earlier provinces of Roman Spain. From 197 B.C. to 27 B.C., the peninsula was divided into two parts: Baetica, "the patrician colony," to the south, with Cordoba as its capital; Lusitania to the west, with Emerita Augusta (Merida) as its capital. Hispani Citerior or Tarra-

TO MERIDA

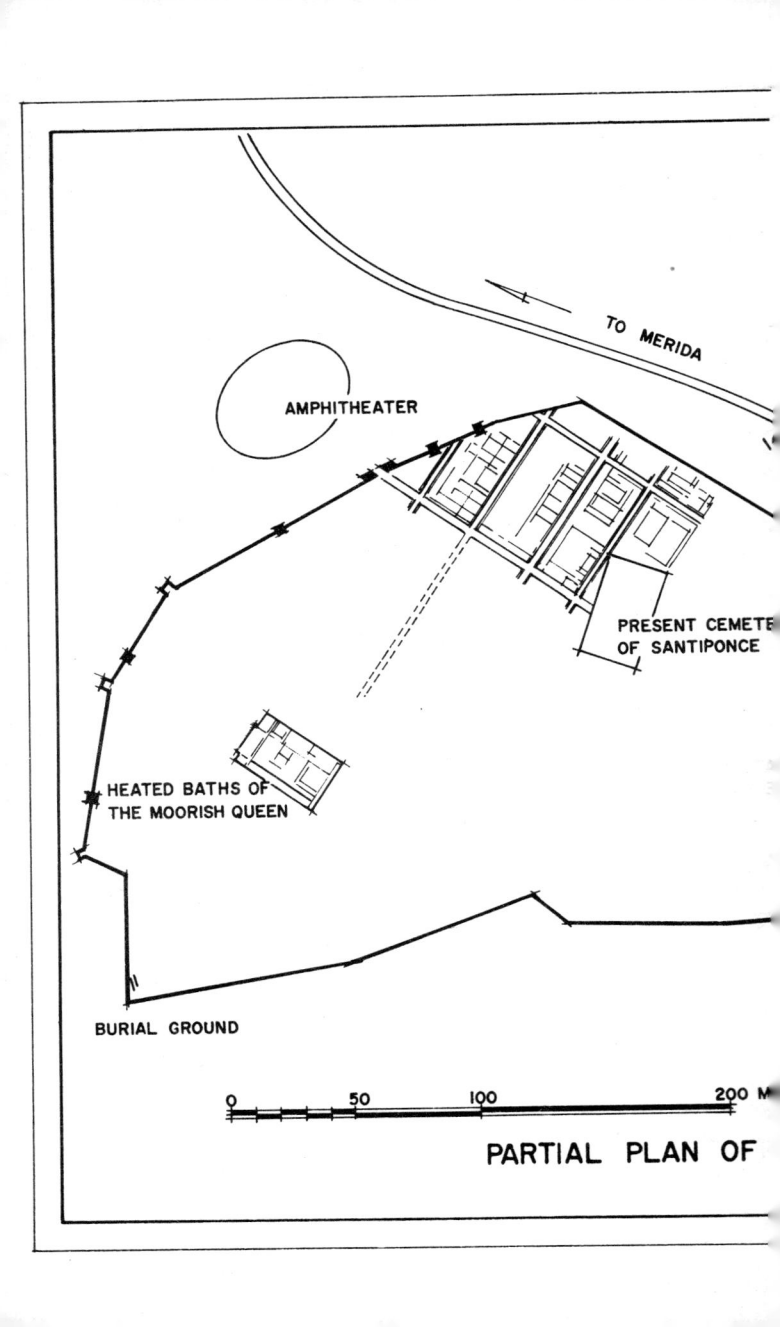

AMPHITHEATER

PRESENT CEMETERY
OF SANTIPONCE

HEATED BATHS OF
THE MOORISH QUEEN

BURIAL GROUND

0   50   100   200 M

PARTIAL PLAN OF

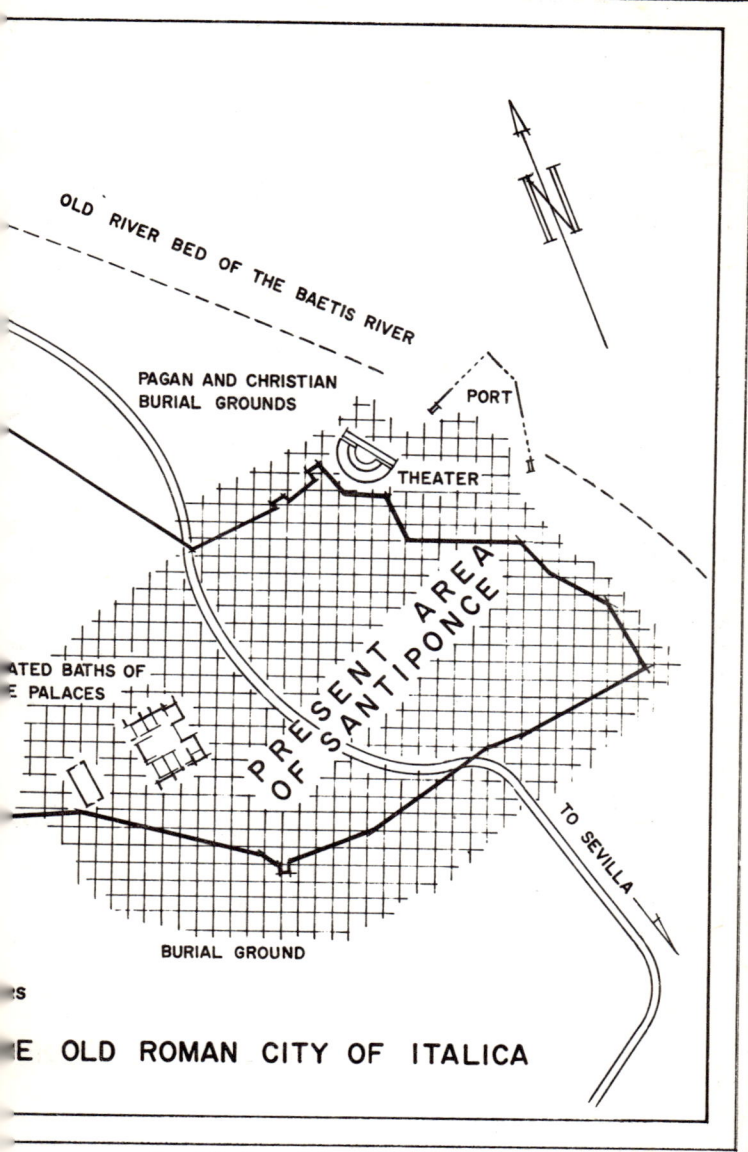

Partial plan of the old Roman city of Italica

ITALICA: THE ROMANS IN SPAIN

conensis, as it was sometimes called, was also partitioned, but not until much later.

In 205 B.C., on the banks of the River Betis, on the site of an ancient Tartessian town, the Romans founded Hispalis (Seville), which was to become a flourishing capital of the province of Baetica. Some vestiges of the Roman occupation can still be seen, including remnants of the walls first thrown up by the Roman founders and rebuilt in 45 B.C. by Julius Caesar and his legions, who came to Hispania to fight the sons of Pompey (at the time being assisted by the native Iberian tribes). In the "Colonia Romula" of Baetica, Caesar made Hispalis his headquarters during his sojourn on the peninsula and affectionately called the city "Civitis Julia" or "Julia Romula."

However, in the earlier years, two centuries before the birth of Christ, Hispalis was outshone by its neighbor about ten miles away—the city of Italica. Italica numbered among the three great Roman cities in Spain, the others being Emerita Augusta and Tarraco, both still thriving cities: Merida and Tarragona. Italica, so elegant and pretentious in its day, can now only be visualized from its imposing ruins, hidden for hundreds of years under the rolling hillocks near the Betis River, its existence forgotten.

Italica was founded in 206 B.C. by the Roman Consul Scipio Africanus the Elder, who gave it the name Vicus Italicensis, in honor of his mother; it shortly achieved the status of a municipality. Romans had long made it a practice to give plots of land to retiring soldiers in recompense for their years of active military service, and Scipio the African rewarded his victorious troops of the Carthaginian Wars by establishing the city of Italica for them. Both legionnaires and their generals made their homes in the newly founded city, giving it much importance from its beginning.

History has always proven man to be incongru-

ITALICA: THE ROMANS IN SPAIN

ous—Scipio and his troops, before embarking on the building of the new city of Italica, had just destroyed another by sacking and burning the Phoenician settlement of Melkarth near the present town of Medina Sidonia to the southeast.

Besides Hispalis, among the Roman settlements near Italica were Oset (San Juan de Aznalfarache), Orippo (Dos Hermanas), Ilipa (Alcala del Rio), Urso (Osuna), Ituci, Olant, Astigis and others. Some of the settlements were built upon sites of earlier cities—however, it is believed by most authorities that Italica was a new city, founded on a previously unsettled site.

The site on which the city of Italica stood is adjacent to the present town of Santiponce, and both here and in the surrounding countryside, other ancient remains of Roman and earlier times have been found, from exquisite sculpted figures (such as the two wondrous Dianas and the lovely Venus) to ordinary Roman pottery, gold bars, and small coins. A measure of Italica's importance can be gathered from the fact that the city minted its own coins, some of which are still occasionally turned up by the residents of Santiponce.

Italica is believed to have been built on seven hills as was Rome and because of this, Italica used the same coat of arms showing the wolf suckling the twins: Romulus, the legendary founder and first king of Rome, and his brother Remus.

Standing on its site today, with only a small portion of the city unearthed, it is difficult to envision Italica at the pinnacle of its glory, but there were numerous temples dedicated to pagan gods, many fine residences, palaces, and public establishments. There was a forum, a hospitum (hotel or inn), a theater, an amphitheater, and aqueducts. Among the most clearly defined ruins are the "termas" (heated public baths). The inn has been identified in the excavations, as well as a bakery and a "tabernae vinaria" (wine tavern). There is much

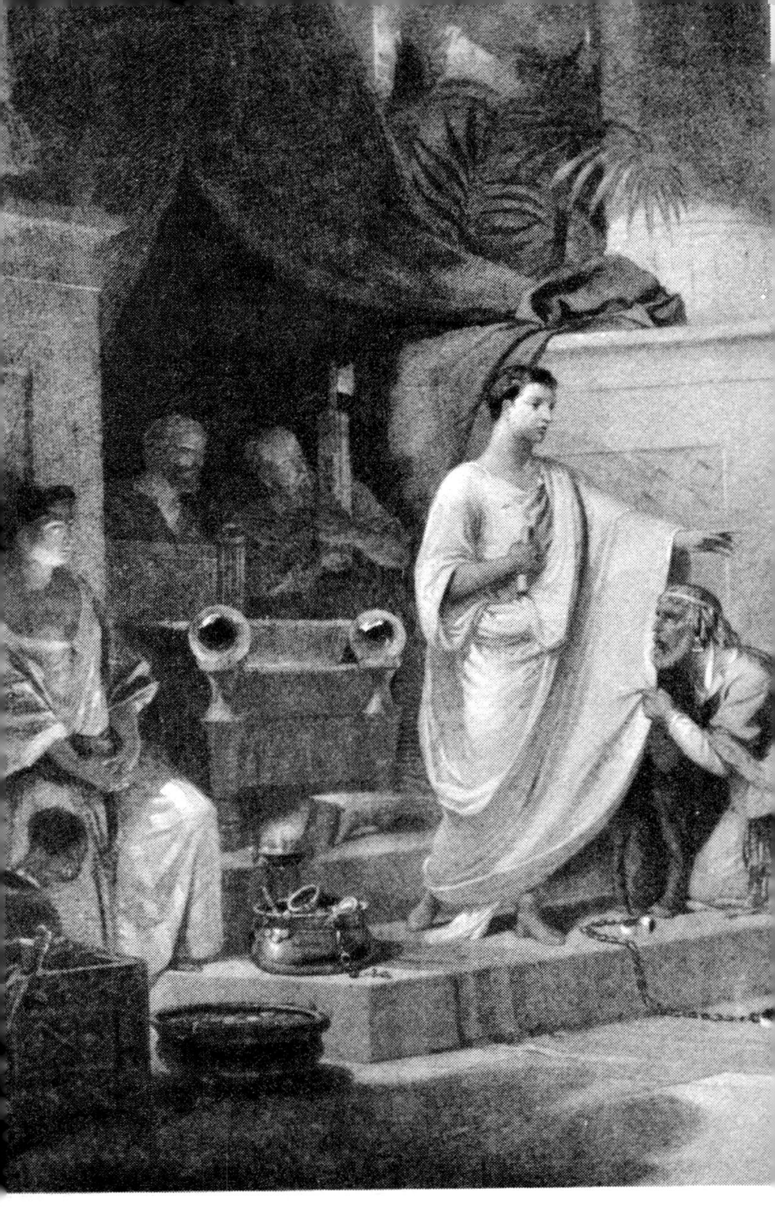

The generosity of Scipio

evidence of the excellent water and drainage systems, still partly operating today.

The baths were constructed in the time of Hadrian (Adrianus), Roman Emperor and native son of Italica who reigned over the empire from 117-138 A.D. An inscription has been found on a piece of lead piping which bears the emperor's name and title: "Imp. C. Had" (Imperator Caesar Hadrianus). Hadrian, whose father and family were from Italica, granted the city the title and rank of "Colonia Aelia Augusta," and favored it with many fine monuments.

The baths were places for meeting and resting. There one learned the latest news and gossip and resolved private and business affairs. There were two sections of equal size, one for men and the other for women. Dressing rooms (apodyteriums), rooms for swimming, and a "hypocaustum" with an oven for steam baths, were all included in the service plan. The baths covered an area of 165 feet by 300 feet. A swimming pool can be clearly traced.

The wide, straight streets of the city were laid out in a symmetrical and orderly plan with regular crossings. The city founders, being legionnaires, laid the streets out squarely as in a typical Roman cantonment, with the "cardo maximum" or principal avenue running north and south. The "decumanus" or second street went from east to west. The streets were paved with large, irregular stone slabs, many twice as wide as those which have been unearthed at Pompeii in Italy. The cardo maximum was eight meters wide and in its center, at a depth of two meters, ran the great sewer which carried away the waste water of the houses and the rainwater overflow. Traces of drainage piping also appear in the secondary streets.

In the center of the city and at the intersection of the main and secondary street was the place occupied by the forum or public hall, the most important build-

ITALICA: THE ROMANS IN SPAIN

ing of the community and the center of city life.

Roman houses were usually one story in height, except in larger cities, which had several stories for renting. The houses had no windows or balconies. The facade was a blind wall, unbroken except for the portico and entrance. Beneath the porticos on the street side were paved walkways approximately four meters wide.

The doorway of a typical Roman home opened on an atrium in which were the statues of the ancestors. Beyond was the tablium (master's study or business office), and the dining halls; then the family's private quarters and bedrooms, the chapel of the household gods, and finally a second columned patio called the peristyle. Some houses also had lateral patios flanking the atrium. From the ruins at Italica, such opulent homes have been clearly traced.

The floors were laid with mosaic in all manner of beautiful designs: geometric patterns, animals, people, gods and goddesses, or other elements dear to the Roman heart. The Emperor Hadrian encouraged the making and popularization of mosaic during his reign. Some of the floors uncovered are still preserved on the site, but others have been moved into palaces and museums in Seville. Some of the finest of Italica's mosaic work are in the palace of the Duchess of Lebrija on Calle Cuna, and others are in the Casa Pilato of the Dukes of Medinaceli. In addition to the mosaic are wonderful collections of statuary, pottery, jewelry, glassware, tools, and other artifacts.

The view looking up the avenue leading to the residential section is reminiscent of Rome with pine and cedar trees in prescribed rows. Today, to the right of the main avenue is an olive grove. At the top of the hill, in a walled enclosure, lies the small cemetery of Santiponce.

Once these avenues were lined with the porticos of great houses and from them issued forth the busy Ro-

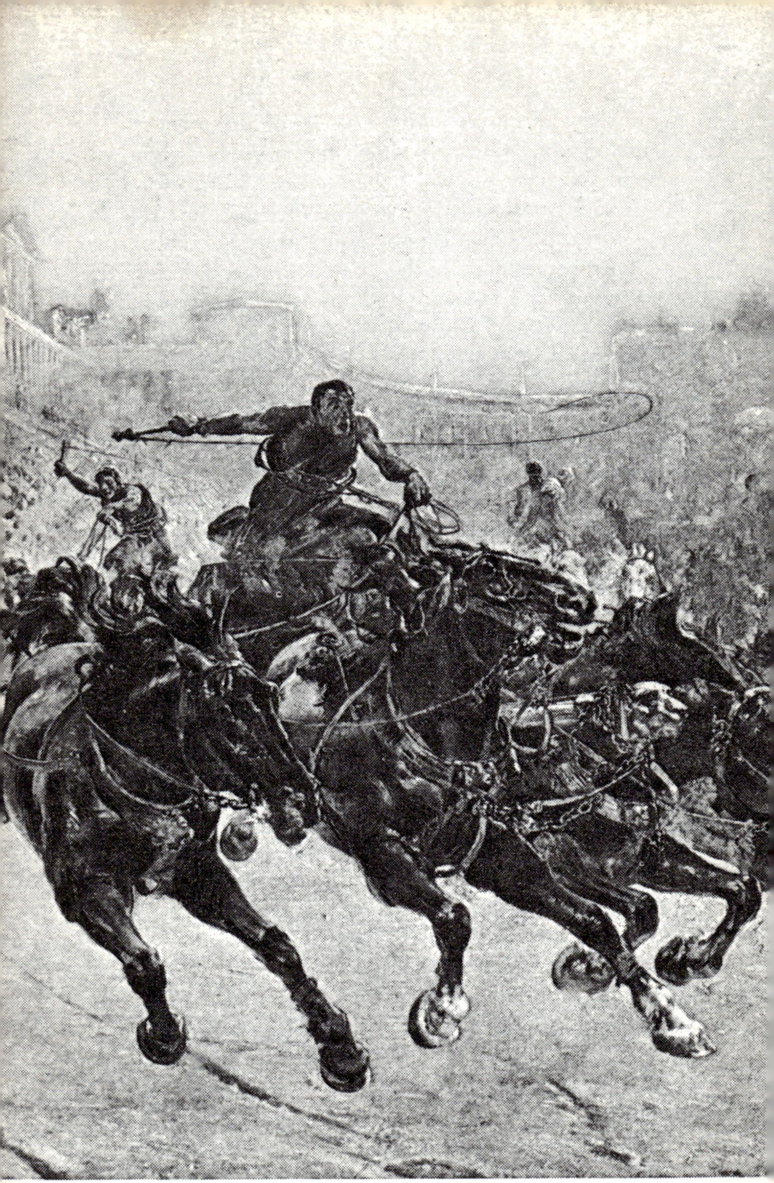

Rome under Trajan—a chariot race

mans. It is easy to imagine the hustle and bustle of a noisy, energetic city, with important citizens moving about in their togas, surrounded by slaves and avid admirers. Less important people, shunted off the sidewalks, would be dodging horsemen or the wheels of passing chariots.

The amphitheater is in the best state of preservation of all the Italican ruins. It is second or third largest in the world, equalled or surpassed only by the amphitheaters which were at Capau, Pozzuoli, and El Djem. Its seating capacity has been estimated at thirty thousand. A comparison can be made by considering that the bullring at Seville today seats about seventeen thousand persons.

Excavations made in the last century by Demetrios de los Rios and the Count of Aguila by order of the Supreme Commission for Excavations and Antiquities in Madrid, together with the excavations carried out in this century, have resulted in an almost complete plan of the amphitheater and its various outlying sections, including the enclosures where wild beasts were kept, and the long tunnel-like corridors beneath the seating areas.

The structure would be in far less ruinous condition had not great pieces of stone been torn away to be used in building work in Santiponce and Seville. Long ago, the magistrates in Seville issued an order, still in existence, that the upper part of the tiers of seats should be pulled down so that the materials could be used. Because of this, the bulk of the construction has suffered considerably. Much of the destruction of other parts of the city can also be attributed to workmen carrying off materials long after the abandonment of the city—which, however, does testify to the excellence of the Spanish stone used throughout the city.

The monumental entrance through which one still passes today had a facade adorned with columns and

ITALICA: THE ROMANS IN SPAIN

statues. The arena is elliptical in shape, around which a racetrack circled. In the center of the oval was a raised platform, rectangular in shape, under which was a pit or vaulted chamber to contain the animals awaiting their turns at events. A low, marble-lined wall around the outer edge of the arena protected the spectators from attack by the beasts. The amphitheater originally had three seating divisions, or extensions, but today only a portion of the lowest remains. There were ten doors which provided access to the seating area.

The first section of seats consisted of six tiers, separated from the next higher section by a passageway. These seats, closest to the arena, were reserved for the nobility or upper class. The seating was divided by stairways into sixteen blocks of tiers, each block opening out to a landing, with an exit door to the corridors underneath. After the section reserved for the magistrates came the "ima cavea," for the "decuriones" (legion officers), then the "media cavea," and above that the "summa cavea" at the highest level, and almost even with the hilltops surrounding the amphitheater, for the common people.

Two large rooms, one on each side of the arena, had direct access to the main corridor, and these were the privileged places for the sponsors of the events or the government officials directing the games.

The contests between the gladiators and beasts were spectacles of peculiar delight to the lusty Romans. Consider their love of excitement: During the time of Nero, the great circus of Rome itself held 380,000 spectators. Consider their capacity for letting of blood (of others!): In celebration of Trajan's triumph in the lower Danube region (now Romania), festivities in Rome lasted for 123 days, during which time 9,000 gladiators and 15,000 wild beasts gave their lives. What libertines the Romans were—what horrors they conceived for entertainment! Though their epoch was the greatest ever known, in time their own excesses destroyed them—more so than the barbarians who came out of the north.

However, as well as avidly enjoying bloodletting and sensual pleasures, the Romans were inveterate theatergoers and there is evidence that a theater existed at Italica. In other Roman theaters in Spain, such as at Merida and Sagunto, dramatic performances have been given in modern times. At Italica, too, on a few occasions the amphitheater has again resounded to theatrical productions. Jose Maria Peman, the beloved Spanish writer, in his book *Andalusia,* tells of the presentation of "Antigona," his own version of Sophocles, with more than four hundred actors parading up and down the stone steps and corridors, proclaiming their verses over the croaking of frogs in the pond in the animal pit. He wrote of the marvelous acoustical qualities of the amphitheater, of sounds which could be heard at distances of 150 meters.

In his delightful way, Peman went on to describe what he called "living archaeology"—the actors who were reviving archaic times. Some of them were recruited for the great choir which represented the people of Tebas (Thebes). Being familiar with "armaos" (impersonators of armed Roman soldiers who march in Holy Week processions), and imbued with the classic aura of the awesome pile of stones wherein they were performing, they strove to enact their roles as Tebans with utmost dignity. At the conclusion of the general rehearsal in the early hours of the morning, it must have been classical indeed to see them in their war helmets and Teban dress, eating their potato omelets and canned sardines, pushing up their gauntlets to peer at their wristwatches, and reverting to their own chopped Andaluz dialect.

In 38 B.C., the Emperor Augustus incorporated Hispania into Rome and declared it a province of the Em-

ITALICA: THE ROMANS IN SPAIN

pire, although there were still a few years of fighting before the stubborn tribes in the north ceased rebelling.

During the first century after the death of Jesus Christ, agriculture in Rome was in a poor state. Many products were exported from Hispania to Rome with Batica providing wine and oil among other staples. The products were shipped in huge amphorae (clay jugs). On broken pieces of these jugs which were found in great refuse piles, were inscriptions which identified the port from which the products were shipped, what the amphorae contained, the date of shipping, name of exporter, and other information. Thus it was established that Italica had been a great business center in the first century. There was, however, a slowdown by the end of the second century when, among other things, the Berbers from Africa were harassing shipping in the straits.

Marcus Ulpius Trajanus (Trajan) was born in Italica on 18 September 52 A.D. and died in 117. He was Emperor of Rome from the year 98 until his death. Triana, the gypsy quarter of Seville, on the banks of the Guadalquivir, was the Tarayana of the Moors and the Trajana of the Romans. Trajan contributed to the great splendor of the city of his birth, as did his successor Hadrian, who some believe was also born in Italica. From the epoch of Trajan and Hadrian came the best part of the fine buildings erected in the area—the amphitheater, the baths, much of the statuary, and other works of art. Hadrian's reign over the Roman Empire lasted from 117 to 138. Cassius states that Hadrian loaded Italica with privileges and favors and during his reign, the Senate raised the city to the rank of colony, giving it the name of Colonia Elia Augusta Italica, all of which suggests that it could have been Hadrian's birthplace.

In 144 A.D. the Roman Consul Lucius Mummius

(Lucio Mummio) gave the city the spoils of war taken in the assault of Corinth in Greece. These trophies, many shiploads of booty, were especially rich in works of art and sculpture. Mummio's gift to the city accounts for some of the original Greek relics discovered in the ruins.

During the reign of Marcus Aurelius (Marco Aurelio), the Stoic philosopher, emperor from 161 to 180 (born 116), the Seventh Legion was based in Hispania because of an invasion from Africa, and Betica was declared an imperial province.

Another personage of note who seems to have been a native of Italica was the poet Silius Italica, although the only evidence in favor of such an assumption is his name.

It has been said that the Spanish-born Roman Emperor, Theodosius I, was a native of Italica, but there is more evidence that he was born in Coca, near Segovia. Theodosius, a great general, was born about 346. He became emperor in 379 and reigned until his death in 395, shortly before the end of the Roman era in Hispania. With the end of the Roman domination, a long and bloody struggle lasting for several centuries was waged against the Germanic tribes.

The Vandals, who gave their infamous name to Andalusia, invaded the peninsula in 409 A.D. For five years, those uncouth barbarians from the north spread wanton terror and destruction over all the land. By great fortune, the Visigoths overthrew the Vandals in 414 A.D. and upheld the new religion of Christianity, along with the Greco-Roman cultural heritages they had been absorbing. The Roman era, though, like those preceding it, was over. Their occupation of Hispania had lasted about six centuries. The first two centuries of Roman rule were marred by sporadic conflicts with the native tribes, but the last four centuries were a period of relatively peaceful coexistence. During the

ITALICA: THE ROMANS IN SPAIN

reign of Augustus, the natives had ceased their struggles against the invaders and had begun to accept Roman culture and way of life.

Rome's contribution to Spain was not only intellectual, but material as well. With their highways, bridges, aqueducts, dams, splendid arches, walls, and cities the Romans were building for eternity. No man could envision that the Roman dream of ruling the world would be shattered because of a child who had been born in Bethlehem during the reign of Augustus —the Child who would be hailed as the Christian Savior.

With Rome's era ended, the Visigoths held sway for a time, then the Moors, and finally the Christians, who with the victory of the Catholic Kings of Granada in 1492, gained control of a united Spain.

In Betica the Visigoths made Hispalis their chief city and as Hispalis gained in prestige and importance, Italica seems to have receded. Early in the eighth century, when the Arab and Berber hordes crossed the Mediterranean straits to conquer Europe, Italica was one of many cities to suffer the horrors of war. The final assault which toppled the Visigoths took place in 711 A.D. and in eight years the Islams, under Tarik, had crossed the Pyrenees into France. During the Moslem occupation a town existed on the site of Italica, and remains of their buildings have been discovered, but Italica was continually plundered. Hispalis, on the other hand, grew in prosperity, favored by the Moslems, who renamed it "Isbilia."

What really happened to Italica? Why was it deserted? There is no certain evidence as to why it was abandoned and left to decay. Memories faded and the ruins strewn with debris slowly covered over the once proud Roman city and its very existence was forgotten. Some believe that the great number of martyrs who lost their lives in the city in the cause of Christianity was responsible for the destruction of the pagan temples, but an otherwise prosperous city could have survived this loss.

The amphitheater has shown signs of an early earthquake which must have taken place after its completion; then in 1255 yet another earthquake destroyed the usefulness of the building. Evidence of other devastating earthquakes has been found and these all must have taken their toll of the city. But the most probable reason for the decline of Italica seems to be the more favorable commercial situation of Hispalis and its rising prosperity with the protection of the Moors.

During the Dark Ages Italica was unknown. It was not until the sixteenth century that the first excavations were begun by two early collectors of Roman antiquities—Don Fadrique Enriquez de Rivera, the first Marquis of Tarifa, and his son, the Duke, Don Perafan de Rivera, viceroy to Naples. Their palace in Seville, called the Casa de Pilatos (said to resemble Pilate's home in Rome) was converted into a museum when these cultivated Sevillian gentlemen brought many fine busts, statues, and other treasures from Rome. These items augmented by their findings at Italica have been preserved by their descendants (the Dukes of Medinaceli) and have been apportioned between the Casa de Pilatos and the Palacio de Madrid. Since 1953, gracious donations have been made by the family to the Archaeological Museum in Seville.

An inestimable debt is owed to the first Marquis of Tarifa and his son for their labors and love of ancient history. Without their interest and knowledge, much that historians and archeologists have been able to discern of the abandoned city of Italica and the Roman occupation of this area would have been lost.

The historian Zuñiga, who wrote in the seventeenth century, tells us that among the treasures brought back from Rome by the Marquis of Tarifa and his son were the ashes of the Italican born emperor Trajan, return-

ITALICA: THE ROMANS IN SPAIN

ing them to the land of his birth. Then Zuñiga goes on to explode our rapture at this exciting development with the information that some curious individual (unnamed) had removed the urn containing the ashes from its column and opened it. The powdery substance that was Trajan puffed up and blew away, scattering all over the garden.

From time to time throughout the centuries, numerous Roman and Greek relics were uncovered in the Italica-Santiponce area and were usually retained by the finders' families, but at the end of the eighteenth century, Don Francisco de Bruna y Ahumada, Alcaide of the Seville Alcazar, with the aid of the Conde del Aguila, made a rich discovery at Italica, which was added to the collections displayed at the Alcazar, a former Moorish palace built on the site of a Roman temple. Now, in addition to being a museum, the Alcazar is the residence of the Chief of State of Spain during his visits to Seville. Many of the treasures which were displayed at the Alcazar were later transferred to the Archaeological Museum, which was constructed in the Plaza de America during the Iberian-American Exposition in 1929. It is there that the largest collection of Italican memorabilia is now housed.

Another magnificent collection of Italican objects is in the palace of the Condessa de Lebrija and her heirs, the Condes de Bustillo, on Calle Cuna in central Seville.

In the late eighteenth century, from 1781 to 1788, Don Francisco de Bruna, in his excavations at Santiponce, uncovered the marvelous torsos of Artemis, Trajan, Hadrian, and an unknown young man. Other important discoveries were made from 1839 to 1842 by Don Ivo de la Cortina and more in 1862 by Don Demetrio de los Rios.

Artemis, the Greek goddess of the hunt, had been adopted by the Romans and called Diana. In Italica there was a temple dedicated to Diana, and in the ruins of this temple, the mutilated image of that divinity was found in the late eighteenth century (1781). This marble statue apparently came from Greece, and the delicate work has led some experts to believe it to be a Greek original dating from the early part of the fourth century B.C. Professor Gomez-Moreno's opinion was that it might be the work of Leocares.

Another authority, Dr. Maria Floriani Squarciapino, however, expressed the belief that the statue is an excellent replica of the famous Diana in Rome, and that it may have been sculpted in Rome and brought to Spain during the second century of our era. Only the torso remains of this statue. Over the Greek garment is a cloak rolled around the waist. At her back, a quiver hangs from a strap which crosses over her body.

The other statue, Diana Cazadora (Diana the Huntress), is considered by some to be a copy of the earlier Greek Artemis. The second Diana, discovered in 1900, is in far better condition. She wears an identical Greek garment with her cloak rolled around her waist. Her head is encircled by a royal diadem, and her hair is drawn to the back of her head. She wears high-laced huntsman boots, and she stands as though holding a spear or bow in her right hand. Both hands of the statue are missing. At her left side is a tree trunk with the skin or hide of a young deer.

This figure of Diana is believed to have been made in Spain by a Roman sculptor, during the second century of the present era, the time of Hadrian or a little earlier. Again Dr. Floriani Squarciapino did not hold with the generally accepted opinion, but believed that both these statues were replicas of an earlier Diana in Rome.

The beautiful statue of Hermes (Mercury of the winged feet) has a place of honor in the Archaeological Museum in Seville. The headless torso was discovered in 1788 in the Italican ruins, with its legs missing. The

ITALICA: THE ROMANS IN SPAIN

right leg was found in 1901 and was attached to the body. The missing portion of the left leg was completed by the Sevillian sculptor, Don Augustin Sanchez Cid, who mounted the statue on its pedestal and placed it in the museum in 1945.

The lovely Venus (Afrodite) of Italica was believed to have been part of the decorations of the theater. Various wonderful statuary and other works of art have been found throughout the years of excavation at the ruins. It is hoped that much more will be uncovered. As is true of all ancient places, Italica is only a trace of what it once was.

Rodrigo Amador de los Rios carried out much work on the excavations around 1862. Houses and various other buildings were discovered and some items of furniture and pieces of masonry have been placed in the Archaeological Museum in Seville and the National Museum in Madrid. It has been possible from his findings and from the results of work of other archaeologists to put together a partial plan of Italica.

During Spain's Golden Age, Rodrigo Caro (1573-1656), prominent son of Utrera near Seville, a poet, folklorist and archaeologist, stirred the imagination of the Spanish people with his elegy "To the Ruins of Italica" (Elegia de Rodrigo Caro, "*A las ruinas de Italica*"). The poem was written as one old Roman to another, lamenting the downfall of the once proud and powerful city. The poignant lines begin: ***"Estos, Fabio, ay dolor! que ves ahora. . . ."***

This, Fabio, what sorrow, that you see now,
Empty fields, melancholy hills,
Where once stood the famous Italica;
Here was the colony of Scipio
The conqueror. . . .

Mankind Is America's Liveliest and Most Beautiful Magazine of History!
Subscribe Now!

Each new issue of Mankind magazine brings you the delight of discovering fresh, bold, unexpected ideas relating to man's adventure on earth. You may join the Knights Templars crusading to free the Holy Land in one article, then thrill to Lord Byron's vision of the glory that was Greece in another. You could visit with Catherine the Great of Russia, travel in the western badlands with Jesse James, explore the London slums of Hogarth's England or battle with Grant at Vicksburg. The writing is lively. The subjects fascinating. The format bold and dynamic. Priceless photographs, authentic maps and drawings and magnificent art in full color illustrate articles written by the world's foremost historians and authors. Mankind is the most entertaining and rewarding magazine you and your family can read. Discover the pleasure of reading Mankind now. Your introductory subscription rate is only $5 for the full 6-issue year.

SUBSCRIPTION FORM • MAIL TODAY

MANKIND PUBLISHING CO., Dept. MKB
8060 MELROSE AVE., LOS ANGELES, CALIF. 90046

Gentlemen: Please enter my subscription to Mankind Magazine for the full subscription year.

☐ **Enclosed is check, cash or money order for $5**
☐ **Please bill me**

Name_____

Address_____

City_____

State_____ Zip_____

MANKIND BOOKS ORDER FORM

MANKIND PUBLISHING CO., Dept. MKB
8060 MELROSE AVE., LOS ANGELES, CALIF. 90046

Please send me the books indicated below for which I enclose $_____ ☐ check, ☐ money order, ☐ cash, payment in full.

CURRENT TITLES @ $1.75 ea.

_____ copy(ies) THE ANCIENT WORLD

_____ copy(ies) GREAT MILITARY CAMPAIGNS

_____ copy(ies) THE AMERICAN INDIAN

_____ copy(ies) THE HUMAN SIDE OF HISTORY

GIFT BOXED SETS @ $6.95 ea.

_____ set(s) ALL 4 BOOKS GIFT BOXED

NOTE: Enclose 25c additional per book to help cover cost of handling and shipping. California residents add 5% tax.

Name_____

Address_____

City_____

State_____Zip_____

GREAT ADVENTURES OF HISTORY

These books, produced in the image of Mankind magazine, provided interesting reading on a variety of fascinating subjects grouped to a singular theme in each volume. You will enjoy reading all books in this series and, in addition, find the varied subject matter, the quality production and visual beauty make these books ideal gifts for any occasion.

CURRENT TITLES IN THIS SERIES.......$1.75 ea.
- THE ANCIENT WORLD (22-001)
- GREAT MILITARY CAMPAIGNS (22-002)
- THE AMERICAN INDIAN (22-003)
- THE HUMAN SIDE OF HISTORY (22-004)

GIFT BOXED SET OF ALL 4 VOLUMES.......$6.95
- ALL 4 BOOKS GIFT BOXED (22-005)